SERVANT LEADERSHIP

by Dr. Jack Schaap

CREDITS
Project Manager: Dr. Bob Marshall
Assistant: Rochelle Chalifoux
Transcription: Cyndilu Marshall
Page Design and Layout: Linda Stubblefield
Proofreading: Rena Fish, Julie Richter, and Maria Sarver

Thank you to my editorial advisor, Mrs. Linda Stubblefield, who has worked many hours to make my thoughts and heart clear to the reader. In January 1977, Linda began working for Marlene Evans with Christian Womanhood. After serving in various capacities, she now serves as the assistant editor of the **Christian Womanhood** *magazine. She is married to David Stubblefield, the academic dean at Hyles-Anderson College. The Stubblefields are the parents of two married adult daughters.*

To order additional books by Dr. Jack Schaap, contact:
HYLES PUBLICATIONS
523 Sibley Street • Hammond, Indiana 46320
www.hylespublications.com
e-mail: info@hylespublications.com

DEDICATION

Dedicated to my associate pastor,

Dr. Johnny Colsten,

"Mr. Servant Leader" of First Baptist Church

I love every day we get to serve together!

In the spring of 1983, I sat in the auditorium of the First Baptist Church and heard, for the first time, a young man preach to whom God would eventually knit my heart. I surrendered to preach under him and asked God for a favor: "If I go into full-time service, could I work for Jack Schaap?" As of this writing, I have either worked for Jack Schaap as a volunteer or as a paid employee for 25 years.

I have enjoyed every moment of my tenure as an employee for him. He has taught me, mentored me, and at times counseled me concerning my family and my future. He has worked side by side with me in the ministry, and he has served me. He has modeled the expression, "I will not use my people to build my work but will use my work to build my people."

Jack Schaap is a pastor, a chancellor, an editor, an author of 17 books, a superintendent of three school systems, a director of a mission board, and he wears many other hats. He still has time to serve those who share in the yoke of the vast ministries of First Baptist Church. Servant leadership is not just a sermon that he has preached or a philosophy he has espoused; it is a garment that he wears.

– Bob Marshall
Assistant Pastor, First Baptist Church

Dr. Jack Schaap is the senior pastor of First Baptist Church of Hammond, Indiana, recognized as one of the largest congregations in America. He has a B.S., an M.Ed., and a D.D. from Hyles-Anderson College in Crown Point, Indiana.

Dr. Schaap counsels approximately 100 church members weekly; he superintends more than 3,000 Christian young people in five separate church-operated, private Christian schools, including one in China. Dr. Schaap is the chancellor of Hyles-Anderson College, a private Bible college which First Baptist Church operates for the purpose of training preachers, missionaries, and Christian educators. For more than 20 years, he preached 35 yearly meetings to tens of thousands of teenagers. First Baptist Church has the largest children's and teens' ministries in America.

Dr. Schaap has been married to his wife Cindy since 1979, and they have two adult children who serve in the ministries of First Baptist Church.

TABLE OF CONTENTS

It is not the critic who counts; not the man who points out how the strong man stumbles, or where the doer of deeds could have done them better. The credit belongs to the man who is actually in the arena, whose face is marred by dust and sweat and blood; who strives valiantly; who errs, and comes short again and again because there is no effort without error and shortcoming; but who does actually strive to do the deeds; who knows the great enthusiasms, the great devotions; who spends himself in a worthy cause; who at the best knows in the end triumph of high achievement, and who at the worst, if he fails, at least fails while daring greatly, so that his place shall never be with those cold and timid souls who know neither victory nor defeat.

– Theodore Roosevelt[1]

INTRODUCTION

In researching the subject of "servant leadership," I soon found a dearth of material. However, I discovered an abundance of books and a wealth of written information on the simple subject of "leadership." I barely scratched the surface of the available material in preparation for the work on this book.

I was moved to action by some of what I studied. I recorded careful and copious notes. I yawned in boredom at some of what I read. I even shook my head in disbelief at some of the "key" leadership philosophies, for I soon found that leadership cannot even be defined!

Decades of academic analysis have given us more than 350 definitions of leadership. Literally thousands of empirical investigations of leaders have been conducted in the last 75 years alone, but no clear and unequivocal understanding exists as to what distinguishes leaders from non-leaders and perhaps more important what distinguishes effective leaders from ineffective leaders.

Definitions reflect fads, fashions, political tides, and academic trends. They don't always reflect reality.[1]

The definitions of leadership were myriad—some simple, some complicated, some to the point. Those who penned the definition—generals, presidents, leadership experts, self-help gurus, and a plethora of others—truly came from all walks of life. Within moments of opening most books, I was confronted with yet one more definition of the 350 available definitions of leadership. Allow me to share a few of these thoughts:

- "Leadership is a long, hard race, run on obscure pathways, not a thrilling spring before a cheering crowd."[2]
- "Every leader is a follower. No one commands an organization without restraints. For every leader, no matter how 'supreme,' there is always a higher authority who must be answered. The Chairman of the Joint Chiefs of Staff is responsible to the Commander-in-Chief. In turn the President of the United States must answer to the Congress and the American people."[3]
- "Leadership is not a matter of command and control."[4]
- "Leadership…is purely subjective, difficult to define, virtually impossible to measure objectively, and cannot be taught in school, any more than a baseball player can learn to throw a curve ball by reading a manual."[5]
- "A leader is *someone who takes us elsewhere.* Someone who becomes a leader doesn't have to have a fancy

title—he or she can be a project manager, a marketing manager, or leader in personnel. But he must leave a legacy of something that would never have been accomplished if he had not done it (assisted by a team, of course)."[6]

- Dwight D. Eisenhower said, "Leadership: the art of getting someone else to do something that you want done because he wants to do it."[7]
- "Leadership is the art of influencing others to their maximum performance to accomplish any task, objective, or project."[8]
- "Leadership is an art, something to be learned over time, not simply by reading books."[9]
- Harry S. Truman purported, "A leader is a person who has the ability to get people to do what they don't want to do and like it."[10]
- "A leader has been described as a person who sees more than others see, who sees farther than others see, and who sees before others do."[11]
- "Leaders are perpetual learners."[12]
- "Leadership is influence—nothing more, nothing less."[13]
- "Leadership is just a matter of understanding who you are and where you want to go."[14]
- "Many people have a narrow understanding of what leadership really is. Say 'leader' and they think general, president, prime minister, or chairman of the board. Obviously, people in those exalted positions

are expected to lead, an expectation they meet with varying levels of success. But the fact of the matter is that leadership does not begin and end at the very top. It is every bit as important, perhaps more important, in the places most of us live and work. Organizing a small work team, energizing an office support staff, keeping things happy at home—those are the front lines of leadership. Leadership is never easy."[15]

- "What is leadership? For years we defined leadership as an *influence process*. In recent years, we have changed our definition of leadership to *the capacity to influence others by unleashing their power and potential to impact the greater good.*"[16]

One shocking truth that stood out in my study was written by LeRoy Eims in 1987 and echoed by many others:

A crisis of leadership engulfs the world. Political leaders, economic experts, editorial writers, newsmen, spokesmen in the fields of education and religion raise the hue and cry: men who know the way and can lead others on the right path are few.[17]

That cry was even taken up by a printing magazine I happened to thumb through. In an article entitled "Electing to Lead," the author stated,

In sports, fans continually argue whether players from

the current era are as good as those who came before them. Was Hank Aaron better than Babe Ruth? Did Michael Jordan have more impact than Wilt? Is Tom Brady the greatest quarterback ever, or did Johnny Unitas long ago cement that legacy? It's a never ending debate to entertain the generations.

Politics is different. How many would suggest any American leader of the last 100 years should have his bust carved into Mount Rushmore? Reagan gains more popularity as the years pass. JFK forever will be filled with promise. FDR showed the way through two of the most trying times in history. After those three, the other 14 presidents since Theodore Roosevelt simply run together.

Does this mean great Presidents exist only in history books? Perhaps today's transparent world, in which every move is instantly analyzed on CNN, written about in blogs, and shared by text message, would make it hard for even Washington, Jefferson, and Lincoln to live up to expectations. Still, one longs to return to a time when leaders exhibited strength, vision, and guidance, and by doing so, truly made this world a better place.[18]

How can we possibly define that which seems to be fast becoming obsolete in our world? These several definitions cannot begin to define the intangibles of leadership—at least how the world perceives leadership. However, tucked away in short chapters or in a couple of paragraphs, I was delighted to find an occasional reference to "servant leadership." Max DuPree said,

"Try to think about a leader, in the words of the Gospel writer Luke, as 'one who serves.' "[19]

When people lead at a higher level, they make the world a better place because their goals are focused on the greater good. Making the world a better place requires a special kind of leader: a servant leader. Two thousands years ago, servant leadership was central to the philosophy of Jesus, Who exemplified the fully committed and effective servant leader.[20]

Servant leadership—little recognized, little known, barely acknowledged—but capable of wielding power and influence beyond belief or human understanding. Servant leadership is revolutionary. LeRoy Eims summed it up this way:

"Christ's teaching regarding leadership continues to have an unfamiliar ring in an age that calls for us to climb to the top. The Bible teaches that to lead is to serve."[21]

*"What keeps people from becoming
servant leaders? The human ego."*
– Ken Blanchard

SERVANT LEADERSHIP

*"Let this mind be in you, which was also in Christ Jesus: Who,
being in the form of God, thought it not robbery to be equal with
God: But made himself of no reputation, and took upon him the form
of a servant, and was made in the likeness of men: And being found
in fashion as a man, he humbled himself, and became obedient unto
death, even the death of the cross. Wherefore God also hath highly
exalted him, and given him a name which is above every name: That
at the name of Jesus every knee should bow, of things in heaven, and
things in earth, and things under the earth; And that every tongue
should confess that Jesus Christ is Lord, to the glory of God the*

Father. Wherefore, my beloved, as ye have always obeyed, not as in my presence only, but now much more in my absence, work out your own salvation with fear and trembling." (Philippians 2:5-12)

Philippians 2:5, which says, *"Let this mind be in you, which was also in Christ Jesus,"* does not necessarily describe Christ's feelings or emotions; rather, this verse describes His mental structure. How did Jesus *think* about His position relative to His duties on this earth? Jesus knew Who He was and what He had to do. Because He knew His position and His purpose, He had to think right to fulfill His purpose.

Luke 6:45, *"A good man out of the good treasure of his heart bringeth forth that which is good; and an evil man out of the evil treasure of his heart bringeth forth that which is evil: for of the abundance of the heart his mouth speaketh."* The heart is key in doing the work of God, and the Christian must have his heart right, tender, yielded, sensitive, and compassionate. However, those strengths are relative to the condition of his mind. I have found that many Christians have wonderful hearts, but they have bad thinking.

Philippians 2:6 shows the path every Christian must walk to have correct thinking. *"Who, being in the form of God, thought it not robbery to be equal with God."* In His thinking, Jesus knew Who He was. He knew that He was the very essence of the Godhead. Colossians 2:9 says, *"For in him dwelleth all the fulness of the Godhead bodily."* Jesus knew He was the Creator God; He knew He was the Creator of the universe. He recognized that He was the Jehovah God of the Old

Testament. Jesus understood very well Who He was.

The words *"…thought it not robbery to be equal with God"* mean that in knowing Who He was, Jesus did not have to prove anything to anyone. Another individual's lack of appreciation of Who He was did not lessen Who He was. Jesus did not come to earth to prove a position to anyone; neither did He come to prove a work. Jesus did not come to prove that He thought He was the Son of God; rather, He came to demonstrate that if He were the Son of God, it would be proven through the way He manifested His works.

Jesus did not often say, "Do you know Who I am?" In Mark 8 after He fed the 4,000, verses 27-29 say, *"…and by the way he asked his disciples, saying unto them, Whom do men say that I am? And they answered, John the Baptist: but some say, Elias; and others, One of the prophets. And he saith unto them, But whom say ye that I am?…."*

When Jesus was taken before Pilate, Matthew 27:11 says, *"…and the governor asked him, saying, Art thou the King of the Jews? And Jesus said unto him, Thou sayest."* Jesus didn't defend His position; in today's vernacular, He would have said, "You said it; I didn't." He was not affirming or denying; His answer was more of a question like, "What do you think?"

Jesus' way of thinking said, "I know Who I am. I don't have to prove Who I am to anyone by what I say. If I truly am the Son of God, watch what I do. *"But made himself of no reputation, and took upon him the form of a servant…."* (Philippians 2:7) Jesus was so secure in Who He was that He could become a servant.

In this chapter, I want to present some Biblical, core ideas about the position of a servant leader as the Bible teaches it. *"But made himself of no reputation, and took upon him the form of a servant, and was made in the likeness of men: And being found in fashion as a man, he humbled himself, and became obedient unto death, even the death of the cross."* (Philippians 2:7, 8)

When Jesus came to earth, He knew He would have to demonstrate His leadership in a certain fashion—not completely by what He said or by the miracles He would perform. He chose a style called "servanthood." He came as a man; He chose humanity. He said, "I will become one of you; I will put on something that few of you wear very well—a garment called 'servant.' By doing so, I will demonstrate, by the way I present Myself to you, the model of leadership I want you to emulate."

> [Jesus'] leadership style is often regarded as one of the most influential and effective the world has ever known. And He did it with twelve inexperienced people! The only person who had much education was Judas, who turned out to be his only turnover problem. Yet, with this ragtag group, Jesus was able to create a lasting impact. Central to Jesus' philosophy was servant leadership.[1]

Leadership starts with how one fashions himself. A careful study of the Gospels reveals Jesus Christ talking to His followers about leadership—especially servant leadership. Mark 10:42-45, *"But Jesus called them to him* [the disciples], *and saith unto them, Ye know that they which are accounted to rule over the*

Gentiles exercise lordship over them; and their great ones exercise authority upon them. But so shall it not be among you: but whosoever will be great among you, shall be your minister: And whosoever of you will be the chiefest, shall be servant of all. For even the Son of man came not to be ministered unto, but to minister, and to give his life a ransom for many." "Servant leadership is the foundation for effective leadership."[2]

1. Bible leadership is servant leadership. "The servant leader is servant first. It begins with the natural feeling that one wants to serve. Then conscious choice brings one to aspire to God. The best test is: Do those served grow as persons; do they, while being served, become healthier, wiser, freer, more autonomous, more likely themselves to become servants?"[3]

2. The world's model for leadership is not a Biblical model. The world has seen multitudes of leaders—from political leaders, spiritual leaders, sports leaders, to Hollywood leaders. Some have been great, but that type of leader is not the Christian's model. Unfortunately, the world does not present the proper model or pattern for leadership. Very few books on leadership can be recommended because they present the world's model of leadership.

We cry out, "Where are the great leaders? The statesmen politicians? Where are the great theologians? The noble men of great leadership who understand their position well? Where are they?"

"Leadership" is a word on everyone's lips. The young attack it, and the old grow wistful for it. Parents have lost it, and police seek it. Experts claim it and artists spurn it, while scholars want it. Philosophers reconcile it (as authority) with liberty, and theologians demonstrate its compatibility with conscience. If bureaucrats pretend they have it, politicians wish they did. Everybody agrees that there is less of it than there used to be. The matter now stands as a certain Mr. Wildman thought it stood in 1648: "Leadership hath been broken into pieces."[4]

However, the direct result of teaching a wrong model for leadership is weakened leadership! Sad to say, too many Christian leaders who are trying to lead consult and copy what the world has to say in their books on leadership. We cannot model that kind of leadership as our pattern. Leadership has nothing to do with a title. Rather, leadership has far more to do with one's sphere of influence.

Leadership is not a position. A promotion has never made anyone a leader. Leadership is a fiduciary calling. The Oxford English Dictionary offers two helpful definitions of fiduciary: "of the nature of proceeding from, or implying trust or reliance"; and "one who holds anything in trust; a trustee."[5]

3. Biblical leadership is not waiting until it is your turn to be in charge; rather, it is proving that you are sufficiently humble to serve. Biblical leadership is having the endorsement of God—not the position of man. Too many Christians desire the position of man without the endorsement of God. A philosophy of life that the world teaches and models and is embraced throughout our Christian circles is "I am bucking up for the next position."

James and John were guilty of this philosophy when they asked Jesus if they could sit next to Him in Heaven. Jesus appreciated their request, but in truth, He knew that they were jockeying for position.

> Jesus exemplified the fully committed and effective servant leader. He sent a clear message on the primary importance of servant leadership when James and John seemed to be vying for a special leadership role among the disciples: *"But Jesus called them unto him, and said, Ye know that the princes of the Gentiles exercise dominion over them…But it shall not be so among you: but whosoever will be great among you, let him be your minister; And whosoever will be chief among you, let him be your servant…."* (Matthew 20:25-27)
>
> The key phrase is *"But it shall not be so among you."* Jesus was talking about a form of leadership very different from the model familiar to the disciples: a leader who is primarily a servant. Servant leadership was to be their mode of operation. And so it should be for all leaders.[6]

In the world, the person who stays faithful long enough will eventually rise to the top. However, organizations occasionally die because sometimes the most unqualified person eventually rises to the top only because he happened to be healthier than his predecessors.

I believe in availability, dependability, and usability, but

the greatest ability is servant ability. One earns the right to
serve. Eventually a position might come when a person has
proven that what he wants is **not** a position. God is looking for
a people who have learned that a position is not what they
want to seek in life. What they seek is the opportunity to make
a difference. The one who serves has attained the highest
position he could ever desire. Biblical leadership is not waiting
until it is one's turn to be in charge, but rather proving that he
is sufficiently humble to serve.

> The way of the Christian leader is not the way of
> upward mobility in which our world has invested so much,
> but the way of downward mobility on the cross. The down-
> ward moving of Jesus is the way to the joy and the peace
> of God, a joy and peace that is not of this world.[7]

4. Serving is not earning the right to lead. Serving is
the choice of Biblical leadership. If one has an opportunity to
serve, he doesn't look at that opportunity as a means to "graduate" to a higher position. The Biblical model is finding a
place to serve and proving oneself worthy of that opportunity.
For example, a church bus driver doesn't look at the bus captain's position and say, "Three more years of driving buses, and
I will have earned the right to be a captain."

No! A bus driver who is a servant leader says, "Maybe in a
few years the leaders will believe they made a good choice
when they asked me to be a bus driver." You never serve for an
opportunity to do what you have always wanted to do. You
serve and then prove by that serving that whoever asked you

to do the job was right in choosing you. Where you serve is an opportunity to show that God knew what He was doing in putting you where you are. In other words, where you are is as high as it gets. If you think there is a higher position, then you have misunderstood servant leadership.

The world's leadership looks at what they are doing as a stair step to get to the next level on the corporate ladder. Servant leadership looks at their job as a way to earn the right to have their job.

5.   Servant leadership magnifies the work that must be done. What impresses God is people who choose to say, "Where is the shovel? What can I do for God's work?" Leadership is saying, "I have a job to do, and my job must be important because God put me here. I have a privilege to prove that a good choice was made when I was chosen for this job." Zig Ziglar said, "The choices you make today will determine what you will have, be, and do in the tomorrows of your life."[8]

6.   Serving is its own compensation. I was walking with one of our security guards, and I stopped to pick up some litter in the alley behind the church. The guard rather seriously asked, "Why do you pick up the litter?"

I jokingly said, "I always need a good sermon illustration. I need to look good!"

He said, "No really, why do you pick up papers?"

I explained, "It is enough for me that it has to be done. That litter just doesn't belong there."

"But it's not your job," he protested. "You don't get paid to be a janitor."

"We don't need compensation to do right. I never want to ask myself, 'Does this fit in my job description?' My compensation comes from picking up litter, putting it in the trash can, and being satisfied with that act of servanthood. I just accomplished something by choice. Serving is its own compensation."

The servant does not have a job description. A servant picks up litter when he sees litter. A servant doesn't care about the position. He cares about the privilege to work. To me, picking up litter around the church property is just as important as preaching in the pulpit of First Baptist Church of Hammond, Indiana. The servant's greatest power is choosing to do work that must be done when nobody else is doing it.

"Servant leadership is empowering rather than demeaning. It is far from servitude or slavery because it is offered out of love rather than out of coercion."[9]

7. Leadership would rather teach by example and partnership than by demand and threat. In Luke 22:28 Jesus said, *"Ye are they which have continued with me...."* Many had forsaken Jesus, but eleven of His disciples had stayed true, and Jesus commended them for continuing with Him throughout His passion, His agony, and His three-year earthly ministry. Jesus taught by example and partnered with His disciples. Albert Schweitzer said, "Example is not the main thing in influencing others; it's the only thing."[10]

Nothing is more frustrating than to work with an individual who hates his job and/or is only putting in his time until he receives a coveted promotion and higher position. The greatest thrill comes from working with people who say, "We have a job to do, and we get to do it together." The greatest privilege of a servant is to work with other people who like to work.

The privilege of Biblical leadership is to do a job and to prove to God that His putting us in a place of service was a good decision. The Biblical model of leadership is Jesus, Who illustrated that going to the top meant going to the Cross and becoming the greatest servant of all.

I did not "arrive" when I was voted in as pastor of First Baptist Church of Hammond, Indiana. I believe I arrived the day I began working at the college and said to myself, "This job is a privilege. Dr. Hyles gave you an incredible opportunity. I hope someday that God and Brother Hyles will believe that I earned the right to have this job they entrusted to me."

People with humility don't deny their power; they just recognize that it passes through them, not from them. Too many people think that who they are is their position and the power it gives them. That's not true. Where does your power come from? It's not from your position; it's from the people whose lives you touch.[11]

Any other concept of leadership is **not** Biblical leadership. If our manner of leadership is not Biblical leadership, then we are not training Biblical leaders to follow us. Instead, we will be training a generation of worldly leaders using the Bible, and we will hurt the cause of Christ.

Wherever you are and whatever you are doing for the

cause of Christ is a great privilege. Prove to God He did right in directing you to where you serve. Perhaps when you have proven that and God sees you as totally humble and satisfied, He might decide to use your abilities and skills in another place of service. If He does, don't see the change as a promotion; see it as just another opportunity to prove that God made a good choice when He gave you a new place to serve.

"Foresight is a characteristic that enables the servant leader to understand the lessons from the past, the realities of the present, and the likely consequence of a decision for the future.
– Ken Blanchard

JESUS, THE ULTIMATE SERVANT LEADER

"Let this mind be in you, which was also in Christ Jesus: Who, being in the form of God, thought it not robbery to be equal with God: But made himself of no reputation, and took upon him the form of a servant, and was made in the likeness of men: And being found in fashion as a man, he humbled himself, and became obedient unto death, even the death of the cross." (Philippians 2:5-8)

In Philippians 2 verses 5 through 8, the pivotal verses in this passage of Scripture, the Bible provides a formula for exercising one's mind. When the Bible says, *"Let this mind be in you,"* the Holy Ghost is saying "Exercise your mind." Exercising one's mind is focused or targeted exercise—much like one lifts weights to concentrate on certain individual muscle sets. The Apostle Paul, under the inspiration of the Holy Ghost, was saying, "Let's target a muscle that is guilty of nonuse. Let's exercise your mind."

Having the availability of the mind of Christ comes with salvation. When a person gives his heart to God, he is not saved by having right thoughts. Salvation does include a process of right thinking, and one has to comprehend some things before he can give his heart to God. The Bible says in Romans 10:10, *"For with the heart man believeth unto righteousness; and with the mouth confession is made unto salvation."* Salvation is a matter of the heart. Growth in the Christian life adds another dimension—the dimension of the mind. A person will never grow much in the Christian life until he starts thinking the right kind of thoughts. Thinking those right thoughts will lead to the right kinds of behavior.

It is important for the believer to give his heart to God. God says we don't get saved by being mentally qualified to get saved. We do have to understand what sin is and that we are sinners. We must understand Who Jesus is and that He is the Son of God. Mental comprehension is understanding that without Christ, we die and go to Hell, but knowing that information still does not get a person saved. Salvation occurs when the heart turns and says, "I believe that!" Our God was so kind and gracious to let salvation be a heart work.

If salvation were mind work, then many people would not qualify because they are not mentally up to speed with God. Once we give our heart to God, He resides inside of us, and He can start helping us with our head knowledge.

Even the brilliant Apostle Paul had to come to a point where he gave his heart. Paul possessed a brilliantly trained Jewish mind, and he was using that mind to arrest Christians in hopes of getting them martyred. God had to get Saul's attention and get ahold of his heart, so He humbled Saul in the dust of a road.

Saul wisely asked, *"Who art thou, Lord?..."* (Acts 9:5) The word for *Lord* is "Sir." He was asking, "Who are You, Sir?"

After the Lord identifies Himself, Saul asks, *"...what wilt thou have me to do?"* (Acts 9:6a) Saul was intelligent enough to give the right answer. Saul had to give his heart to God, and at that moment, his heart was humbled. Fourteen years later the Apostle Paul began doing the work of Christ when he wrote his first epistle, probably Galatians.

By carefully reconstructing the outline of history, one will find that Paul spent three years in the Arabian Desert, quite possibly at Mount Sinai where God gave Moses the laws. He was receiving tremendous insight on how the law of God for the Jew would make it possible to lead all men to Christ. The law is a schoolmaster to lead men to Christ.

Paul also spent several years at the church of Antioch as a

humble servant, where he learned to give his heart to God. To be sure, Saul had already received quite an education before he got saved, and afterward he received an additional 14-year education by the Lord Himself as well as by some scholars at the church in Antioch. In writing the book of Philippians, Paul tells the reader that he too must give his heart to God.

Allow me to share the kind of mental thinking that the Apostle Paul, in his dedicated heart, said we must have in order to grow as a Christian and likewise to become a competent leader, father, pastor, teacher, etc.

As I have already stated, the Apostle Paul said, *"Let this mind be in you, which was also in Christ Jesus."* (Philippians 2:5) We must work to get our mind in the same shape as was the mind of Jesus.

"Who, being in the form of God, thought it not robbery to be equal with God" refers to servant leadership and the developing of skills to lead a home, to lead a business, to lead a family, to lead a Sunday school class or a bus route, or to lead a ministry. In whatever leadership role God has given to us, we must strive for servant leadership. *"Who, being in the form of God…"* means "Jesus Christ, Who being in the shape or the very nature of God did not command or demand that He seize control or that He take by force that which seemed to be similar to what God is or that which He knew absolutely He was already intrinsically. In other words, Jesus had not yet been recognized by anyone for Who He was; nobody knew Who He was. Before Jesus Christ came to earth, the prophets wrote about a coming Messiah, but when Jesus Christ came, none of

them recognized him. The Bible says in John 1:11, *"He came unto his own, and his own received him not."* It is not that they weren't looking for a Messiah; nobody knew that Jesus Christ was the Creator God. Jesus knew where His future would be; He knew what glory awaited Him. He knew that every created being—not just man, but every bird, every insect, every mammal, every reptile, every creature that draws breath will say, *"…Blessing, and honour, and glory, and power, be unto him that sitteth upon the throne, and unto the Lamb for ever and ever."* (Revelation 5:13) Every created creature will someday say "Glory to God" in a language God understands!

The Son was the Creator God—the very fullness of the Godhead—and He bodily expressed that He was born as a baby in a manger. He exhibited and manifested servant leadership though He understood His future exaltation. He created everything in the animal kingdom and then created man in His own image. He created everything knowing that all of creation would join together in a magnificent chorus orchestrated by His choir of angels and all the redeemed of Heaven singing.

In going to earth, unknown and unrecognized by everyone as to Who He really was, Christ demonstrated to mankind how they could fully reach their potential. How then does one obtain his greatest potential?

1. Develop your mind (or exercise your mind) to understand that Christ knew and felt as God. Jesus knew where He was going, but the way to get there was not how most people thought. A servant leader does not feel it is necessary to push or promote himself to gain what he knows he is capable of being. The great comprehension of Philippians 2:6 is Jesus' teaching that we do not need to push or promote or grab or seize. *"Who, being in the form of God, thought it not robbery to be equal with God."*

At an American Management Association conference for presidents, an invited speaker in all seriousness said, "I want men that are vicious, grasping, and lusting for power." He also gave his version of the Golden Rule—"He who has the gold makes the rules."[1]

What an antithesis to the way Jesus looked at leadership! Even in knowing Who He was and understanding that His future was to be identified as God, Jesus knew He did not have to seize power; He didn't have to prove anything to anyone. He knew that it would eventually come to Him.

Jesus was saying, "Let it come to you; don't go to it." Consciously say, "I will let it come to me when it is time to come to me." Do not feel it necessary to push or promote yourself to gain what you know you are capable of being.

I went through a terrible struggle in my late twenties over this very matter. The struggle was knowing what I believed I was capable of becoming and knowing and believing that Almighty God had called me to preach. I went to college and trained to become what I believed I was capable of becoming. I had a ministry, but I believed it was not matching what I thought God wanted from me. I wrestled with that knowledge to the point where it almost drove me crazy because I simply could not analyze the situation in my mind. I never talked to anyone about my dilemma, and I now wish I had talked to my father-in-law, Dr. Jack Hyles. Instead, I went through a private hell for several years just wrestling in my mind about why God's call was not becoming a reality. I now know that what God was doing was making me learn this principle. I discovered that God knew where I was, and God knew how to get me where I had to go. Every Christian has to learn this lesson.

2. Empty yourself—pour yourself into what you are doing. Philippians 2:7 which says, *"But made himself of no reputation…"* simply means "He emptied Himself."

We must pour ourselves into what we are doing. Nobody will become what he should become unless he gives himself to the work. A person becomes that to which he gives himself. Acts 6:4 says, *"But we will give ourselves continually to prayer, and to the ministry of the word."* What happened when some people gave themselves to prayer? The church exploded in growth. God brought the increase!

Jesus didn't go to earth to prove to everyone that He was God. He went to earth to empty Himself of everything and to pour Himself into His mission on earth. He poured Himself into the blind, the crippled, and the needy until the crowds were so great He had to tell the people He was healing and helping not to tell anyone else about Him.

He didn't say to blind Bartimaeus, "Do you know Who I am? I am Jesus the Son of God."

No! He said, "Shhh, don't tell anyone."

Too many people seek for an opportunity. They beg to ask,

"Does anyone recognize how great I am? Does anyone recognize how wonderful I am?"

Jesus did exactly the opposite of what most people seek to do. If anyone had a right to say to people, "I just healed you. Do you know Who I am? Then tell everyone Who I am because it would be good for the people to know that the Son of God is walking among them," it was Jesus. Not so with Jesus! He had to leave the area because He could not keep the people quiet about His miracles. By pouring Himself into His earthly ministry, He was exalted to the position where in the kingdom of God He was greatly used. Wherever you are, pour yourself into what God has given you. If you don't pour yourself into that, you will never get to the rest of your life. You must pour yourself into what you are doing right now. You pour yourself into where you live and the people with whom you have influence.

One man said to me, "I know I am supposed to be the pastor of a church, but my wife won't let me."

I answered, "My brother, you have missed your calling. Don't misunderstand me. God probably has called you to pastor a church; I am not disputing that call. But the Bible says in I Timothy 3 that you are supposed to pastor your wife and your family. If you cannot pastor your wife and family, then you are not qualified to pastor a larger church. If you cannot get your wife to follow you, why do you think God would give you a congregation of people to follow you?"

If I can be so "earthy," I pastor two churches—First Baptist Church and my wife. I believe the most important one to pastor is my wife. I pray more and work harder on pastoring my wife because I believe that being a husband is one of the greatest challenges of Christianity. We are told to love our wives in three ways, and the first way is like Christ loved the church. Women are never commanded to love their husbands, but the husband is commanded to love his wife like Jesus loves.

If I can learn to love my wife like Jesus loves the church, that is incredible love. Then loving my church people becomes far easier. However, many men do not want to learn the lesson of "I will pour myself into my wife." I have found if I pour myself into my wife, then God will exalt me.

Too many people spend their lives unhappily waiting for the "big event" to take place when the big event is already here—right now, right where you are with what you have. It is not where you are not, with those whom you do not know. You pour yourself into what you have, and God will exalt you way beyond what you can imagine.

"To serve God, we must serve others, as Jesus did."
– LeRoy Eims

THE STEPS TO BECOMING A SERVANT LEADER

I believe in following men. Paul said, *"Be ye followers of me, even as I also am of Christ."* (I Corinthians 11:1) He qualified that statement by adding, "I follow Christ." I believe a person will never reach his potential until he finds a man of God who has yielded his will to a man of God, and he yields his will to the will of that man of God.

We must find someone who has learned to do what he is supposed to do and does it. However, in following men, we sometimes tend to pick up their idiosyncrasies. For instance, Dr. Jack Hyles had an esophagus problem that caused him to cough and clear his throat often. Some college students chose to copy that idiosyncrasy of Brother Hyles as if that was where the power of God came from. We must always follow the pattern of Christ. Dr. Hyles often thundered from the pulpit of First Baptist Church, "Don't copy the copy. Copy the original." Our pattern is Jesus Christ.

"Let this mind be in you, which was also in Christ Jesus: Who, being in the form of God, thought it not robbery to be equal with God: But made himself of no reputation, and took upon him the form of a servant, and was made in the likeness of men: And being found in fashion as a man, he humbled himself, and became obedient unto death, even the death of the cross." (Philippians 2:5-8) Philippians 2 is called the great *kenosis* hymn, a song of humility for the Lord Jesus Christ. *Kenosis* is a Greek word meaning "self-emptying," which is derived from the phrase *"made himself of no reputation."*

Servant leadership is so contrary to the leadership the world establishes. When we find genuinely good, strong leadership in any avenue, someone has stumbled across the teaching of servant leadership.

Someone gave me the book entitled *The Disney Way of Doing Things*. As I paged through the book, I immediately thought, I have a Book like this. It is a little thicker, and it is called the Holy Bible. My point is that any company striving for good leadership has someone somewhere in the organization who catches the powerful philosophy of servant leadership. Disney may be a great business; but God's business is the greatest business in all the world. Therefore, God's work should be done better than any other business in the world.

THE STEPS OF RIGHT THINKING IN SERVANT LEADERSHIP

1. **Jesus Christ knew Who He was and did not need to impress anyone to prove Who He was.** Because Jesus knew He did not need to impress anyone, He could begin the humbling process needed for being a servant leader. Step one in the humbling process for the Christian is learning he does not have to impress anyone with his position, title, or rank. In his book *Developing the Leaders Around You: How to Help Others Reach Their Full Potential*, author John C. Maxwell astutely noted,

> When it comes down to it, titles are worth little. A lofty title doesn't help a poor producer. A lowly title doesn't hinder a super producer. Position, like title, doesn't make a leader either.[1]

Psalm 75:6 and 7 says, *"For promotion cometh neither from the east, nor from the west, nor from the south. But God is the judge: he putteth down one, and setteth up another."* God is the One Who gives promotion, position, title, and achieved rank. If God gave that promotion, then no man can take it away. We need not be afraid to humble ourselves; we must though if we are to see the importance of the work God has for us.

2. **Jesus had to go through an emptying process.** The

phrase *"...made himself of no reputation"* means Jesus "emptied Himself" or poured Himself into the work He was called to do. Jesus was not called to a position, nor was He worried about a position. He was called to do a work. *"For the Son of man is come to save that which was lost."* (Matthew 18:11) Jesus had to be careful about how popular He became because He was illustrating that His work was not about popularity; it was about His work. He did not pour Himself into promoting Himself; He poured Himself into His work.

3.   Jesus took on the form of a servant. *"...and took upon him the form of a servant...."* (Philippians 2:7) The word *servant* in the Greek is *doulos* meaning "bond servant." Someone has either voluntarily or involuntarily given himself to another person; they are knit together. That word *knit* means "to join closely or unite securely." A servant is someone who not only has forgotten about who he is and is pouring himself into the work, but now he has knitted himself to the cause to which God has called him. A servant has two requirements.

•   *Self-discipline.* Servants are the most disciplined people in the world. Why? It is impossible to give what you don't control. You cannot give what is not yours to give, and you cannot give what is not controlled by you to give. The most disciplined One Who ever lived was Jesus Christ. Nobody possessed a more impeccable level of character than did Jesus Christ. Isaiah 50:7 says, *"...therefore have I set my face like a flint...."* His was a disciplined life. If you want to be a servant, forget about who you are or who you aspire to be, pour yourself into your work, and be a self-disciplined servant.

•   *Submission.* The Bible says that a servant is someone who submits to another's will. The most disciplined people are the only ones who are qualified to submit to someone else's will. The mark of a servant is not simply his service or his attitude; rather, it is his willingness to submit.

A wife says, "I refuse to give myself to my husband because he…." An employee states, "I refuse to give myself to my employer because he…." Anyone can find fault with another person, and the person who seeks to find fault with others shows a lack of self-discipline. Do you not think that Jesus Christ could have found fault with the people He served? Do you understand the Son of God was perfect, yet He submitted Himself to human beings? Jesus submitted to the arrogant, opinionated, proud, self-righteous Pharisees and Sadducees of the Sanhedrin because He knew they were chosen by God to send Him to the Cross—His greatest earthly work.

The Bible is filled with examples of men who were singleminded in their walk with God. But the greatest example is Jesus Himself. *"And it came to pass, when the time was come that he should be received up, he stedfastly set his face to go to Jerusalem."* (Luke 9:51) His men saw this and were amazed. And why were they amazed? Because He knew exactly what awaited Him and marched forward without flinching.[2]

Jesus forgot about Who He was, poured Himself into His work, made Himself of no reputation, and was so disciplined that He submitted to those who least deserved it. Jesus came to do the work of His Father. Under the inspiration of the Holy Ghost, Paul is saying, "This is the kind of man to be." *"Let this mind be in you, which was also in Christ Jesus."* (Philippians 2:5)

Wife, the next time you don't want to listen to your husband; employee, the next time you don't want to listen to the boss; teenager, the next time you don't want to get along with someone, simply say to yourself, "I wonder how Jesus felt when He had to endure the enmity of some cheaply paid, conscripted Roman guards who were lusting for blood, hitting Him in the face because they had nothing better to do." They pummeled His body, and He put up with their attack and submitted Himself. He submitted Himself—to death.

The wording in the Greek does not mean that He submitted Himself to an act of dying. He submitted Himself to a power that He had created. Death is a power. Though death does not have a tangible body, it is just as real as a human body. Jesus submitted Himself to everything He wasn't because death is everything God is not. *"…I am the resurrection, and the life: he that believeth in me, though he were dead, yet shall he live."* (John 11:25) Jesus was saying, "Death, what can I do for you?"

Death had the humiliating death of the Cross for Him, and Jesus submitted Himself to that shameful, humiliating death. The mark of a servant is not simply his service or his attitude, but rather to whom or what he is willing to submit. Jesus was incredibly willing to submit Himself to people and to opportunities that most would ignore.

Mankind desperately needs to grasp the idea of servitude. A Christian will never know the full, complete opportunities

He has in God's will until he is willing to say to anyone, "If that is what you need, I am your man." That is servant leadership.

4. Jesus Christ showed Himself a man. *"...and was made in the likeness of men: And being found in fashion as a man...."* Jesus was a living, Scriptural demonstration of genuine manhood. Real manhood says, "I am strong enough to do whatever has to be done. I am willing to submit myself." David told Solomon to be strong and "show thyself a man."

Jesus came onto the stage resembling men. Jesus left Heaven to walk on earth, and in so doing, He made a statement of manhood. He said, "In case you care to look, I am going to show you a demonstration of Scriptural manhood."

5. Jesus humbled Himself. Because He was a man, He demonstrated what a Biblical man is. Verse 8 says, *"And being found in fashion as a man, he humbled* himself...." *Humbled himself* means "lower your rank further still." "The Christian tradition has often viewed humiliation as a deepening and purifying process, with Jesus as the primary model of suffering humiliation with extreme grace."[3]

One day when I still worked at the college, I noticed a spill that had not been cleaned up, so I got a bunch of rags and was cleaning it up when a junior administrator came into the room and asked me why I was cleaning it up.

"Because it is here," I answered, "and someone needs to clean it up."

"You know who you are," he said. "You will be the next pastor of First Baptist Church, so why bother?"

"First, I don't know that I'm slated to be the next pastor of First Baptist Church, and secondly, if I am, I had better earn that position." I stood up, looked him in the eye, and said, "The last thing people want or need is an arrogant pastor who is too big for a job like this telling them what to do."

"God measures people by the small dimensions of humility and not by the bigness of their achievements or the size of their capabilities."[4] Far too many Christians are a long way from humility. Humility is not just bowing on a knee. Humility is a series of choices including submitting to all people, including unlovable people. George Washington Carver succinctly addresses a person's attitude toward his fellow man:

> How far you go in life depends on your being kinder with the young, compassionate with the aged, sympathetic with the striving, and tolerant of the weak and the strong because someday in life you will have been all of these.[5]

Only when we have submitted ourselves to all men have we met the qualifications to say, "I believe I have earned the right to show humility." No wonder God hates pride so much! True humility is so far removed from those of us who think we are humble—especially from those who *know* they are. *Humbling* means "lowering your rank and having a modest opinion of oneself. Humility is not self-deprecation—saying, "I am nothing." Humility means devoid of haughtiness. Humility is behaving in an unassuming way. Charles H. Spurgeon said, "Humility is to make a right estimate of one's own self."

6. Jesus modeled obedience. Verse 8 says, *"And being found in fashion as a man, he humbled himself, and became obedient...."* My predecessor, Dr. Jack Hyles, often taught that the most important principle parents can teach their child is to obey. Teaching a child obedience can be very difficult because a child wants to insist on being who he is. "I have my rights," he asserts. That child will have to humble himself in order to truly learn how to obey.

Hebrews says Jesus Christ learned obedience through that which He suffered. *"Though he were a Son, yet learned he obedience by the things which he suffered." (Hebrews 5:8) Suffering* is "what you are willing to put up with to do what God expects you to do." How far would you go to obey? Jesus showed how far He was willing to go to obey. He poured Himself into the work of Calvary. He humbled Himself and lowered Himself because He knew He could not lift up anyone unless He was beneath them. Jesus went down lower than low and lifted up the whole world!

A life of obedience by the leader is the greatest motivation to the people who follow him. They see his life and are challenged to greater heights of commitment and obedience."[6]

Philippians 2:9 continues, *"Wherefore God also hath highly exalted him...."* Having the mind of Christ leads to obedience, and obedience is the ultimate act of humility, which comes from self-discipline and submission. Jesus Christ was the most obedient person who ever trod this earth. Whom did He obey?

The Bible says in Philippians 2:8 that He *"...became obedient unto death, even the death of the cross."*

Only when we have embraced these six steps leading to obedience have we reached the place where God can teach us servant leadership.

"Criticism, as it was first instituted by Aristotle,
was meant as a standard of judging well."
– Samuel Johnson

COMPREHENDING CRITICISM

"Whoso is simple, let him turn in hither: as for him that wanteth understanding, she saith to him, Come, eat of my bread, and drink of the wine which I have mingled. Forsake the foolish, and live; and go in the way of understanding. He that reproveth a scorner getteth to himself shame: and he that rebuketh a wicked man getteth himself a blot. Reprove not a scorner, lest he hate thee: rebuke a wise man, and he will love thee. Give instruction to a wise man, and he will be yet wiser: teach a just man, and he will increase in learning. The fear of the LORD is the beginning of wisdom: and the knowledge of the holy is understanding." (Proverbs 9:4-10)

This chapter is the direct result of talking with a pastor and his wife who have served at the same church for two decades. This good man has built a blameless ministry and has tried to walk circumspectly and to live above reproach and criticism. However, an attack did come, and it came from the people whom they knew and loved. The attack did not come from an enemy; the attack came from within. The Psalmist said in Psalm 41:9, *"Yea, mine own familiar friend, in whom I trusted, which did eat of my bread, hath lifted up his heel against me."*

"Loyalty, very simply, is the desire to help other people become successful."[2]

I hate to see anyone fall victim to criticism, but it will inevitably happen. What do you do when someone criticizes you? "All leaders get criticized. It's their response to criticism that sets them apart."[1]

After this conversation, I penciled some thoughts about the matter of criticism. Proverbs 9:7 says, *"He that reproveth a scorner getteth to himself shame...."* For those who want to confront the person spreading criticism, be mindful of this verse! A scorner is someone who is very smooth and very purposely charts out his criticism in order to gain the affection and loyalty of other people. A scorner brings a negative shadow over someone, and that someone is almost always an authority figure. The Bible says not to bother reproving or correcting the scorner because if you try to reprove or correct a scorner, he will hate you. In other words, reproof will just ratchet up the criticism or pour gasoline on a fire.

Proverbs 9:8 teaches the difference between a scorner and a wise person. *"Reprove not a scorner, lest he hate thee: rebuke a wise man, and he will love thee."* Still, even good people sometimes get caught in the negative listening mill. Even though they don't necessarily believe the rumor mill, they still listen to the talk. Sometimes they even repeat what they heard—without the malice of the scorner. That situation needs to be addressed by a leader. A wise leader must make a judgment call about whether or not he should expend the time to try to help the person who passes on negative reports. Some wise people will readily accept correction and even love the one who is doing the correcting. *"Give instruction to a wise man, and he will be yet wiser...."* (Proverbs 9:9) The Bible promises that the one who accepts correction will become wiser and wiser; he will increase in learning.

Based on these Scriptures, allow me to share some principles about the matter of dealing with unearned or undeserved criticism.

> "Get a friend to tell you your faults, or better still, welcome an enemy who will watch you keenly and sting you savagely. What a blessing such an irritating critic will be to a wise man."
> – Charles Spurgeon

1.   **Many Christians feel that criticism and slander can be avoided simply by consistent Christian living and having an even-tempered spirit.** They can't. The one who chooses to do a standout work for the cause of Christ or to be righteous and obedient will invariably come under attack. "People of honor, people of their word, people who try to live in purity of mind and heart—such individuals stand out, if only because of

their relative scarcity."[3] One reason why so many people—teenagers included—do not take a strong stand for Christ is not that they are not potentially strong people. They do not want to be pointed out as being different. They do not realize that taking a stand is a part of the turf of success.

The person who is making progress and going forward will automatically stand out. That forward progress is called righteousness or success. The person who is building a big ministry or a big bus route or winning records—whether it be in sports or in soul winning—will be criticized. The nature of sinful man is to learn something he doesn't like about the person out in front and criticize him.

Criticism says, "I recognize he is a standout in that area, and I have to find some reasons why I am not there." The bottom line is that there is no way to live so good that when you do good, it will not be criticized.

Critics do not need a reason to criticize. They criticize because they are critics by spirit and by nature. The scorner does not need an excuse to be scornful; he scorns because he is a scorner. The person who works hard, is sincere, and experiences a measure of success in his Christian life will become a target as soon as his ministry appears on the radar screen of the critic. Anyone who is succeeding for the Lord or trying to build a successful work for the Lord will come under the scrutiny and the scorn of the critics.

2. Only one person has ever been psychologically adjusted, emotionally mature, and spiritually perfect on this earth—our Lord Jesus Christ. In His perfection He was nonetheless highly scorned and criticized—almost exclusively by the religious crowd. As perfect as He was, as gifted as He was, as mature as He was, as psychologically stable as He was, as mentally competent as He was, as spiritually discerning as He was, as infinitely compassionate as He was, and as unbelievably loving as He was, He was still hung on a cross and crucified. The more perfect one is, the more imperfection cannot stand that perfectness.

The better an artist is at his art, the more criticized he will be by those who think they are artists but don't have the caliber or quality he does. Gifted athletes are criticized by less-gifted athletes who wish they were as gifted, but aren't. The more gifted one is in his craft, the more he will be criticized. That criticism is the nature of sinful man.

The people who most viciously criticized Jesus were those who religiously thought they were on His spiritual level, but they weren't. Critics are those who perceive when another steps out of his league and are bothered by his growth. Any kind of distinguishing act will generally bring criticism.

Criticism could come for your dress, your speech, your looks, your manner of carriage, or your maturity around adults. It could be because you are cool under pressure, or it could be for any number of skills or abilities. Dawson Trotman said, "There is a kernel of truth in every criticism. Look for it, and when you find it, rejoice in its value."[4] The bottom line is the more "perfect" you are in a given area, the more you will be criticized.

3. Those who desire to achieve certain positions of

office should have a good reputation. For instance, I Timothy 3:1 says, *"…If a man desire the office of a bishop, he desireth a good work."* The Bible is saying that desiring a position of helping other people do something is good. Nothing is wrong with saying, "I would like to step up as a young man and set an example among my peers." There is nothing wrong with saying, "I would like to generate a spirit of enthusiasm in our school this year." The Bible says that any time a person wants to step up and influence people for righteousness, he desires a good thing.

However, that passage in I Timothy 3 comes with some qualifiers. Verse 2 says, *"A bishop then must blameless…."* The word *blameless* means that if one is accused, there is no evidence to support the accusation. It will all be hearsay evidence. Being *blameless* means not giving the accusers any grounds or not validating the criticism of the disputants.

I Timothy 3:2-7 continues, *"…the husband of one wife, vigilant, sober, of good behaviour, given to hospitality, apt to teach; Not given to wine, no striker, not greedy of filthy lucre; but patient, not a brawler, not covetous; One that ruleth well his own house, having his children in subjection with all gravity; (For if a man know not how to rule his own house, how shall he take care of the church of God?) Not a novice, lest being lifted up with pride he fall into the condemnation of the devil. Moreover he must have a good report of them which are without…."* When a man accepts a leadership position—specifically in a local church—the Bible does not say that man has to have a good report of those **within**. The Bible says that from within, he must be **blameless**. If someone decides to criticize the pastor, the man of God must not pro-vide the attacker with one shred of evidence to support his attack. Neither can he stop the criticism. He must be blame-less. Being blameless means that when the critics attack, no evidence can be found to support that criticism nor can a flaw be found with the character of the one being attacked.

The bankers, the businessmen, the legal people in the Hammond area should think that First Baptist Church of Hammond, Indiana, is impeccable. They might not like our message, but our reputation should be such that people can say about the members of First Baptist Church, "They are honest, hard-working people with incredible character. I can't stand their religion, but I can't find a fault with them." What often happens in Christianity is that the community praises the man of God, but the crowd on the inside harasses him because of his righteous stand.

With the Christian crowd, Christians must be blameless. Even when diligently hunting for evidence, other Christians should not find one shred of support for what they do not like. The Bible says in this passage that those who are without bet-ter have a good report; those who are within should not be able to validate any criticism. What is the Bible saying? If you are a standout, you will probably be criticized by the crowd with whom you run. Leading people and caring for them will more than likely bring criticism sooner or later.

Oftentimes criticism comes to leaders when they must reprove or rebuke followers or even when motivating them. The leader may have to stomp his foot and say, "We can do this! I expect better from you than that!" Perhaps he stepped on the toes of his people in a sermon, and now they are "barking" about his words. It is very probable that a leader will be criticized within the ranks of those whom he leads.

4. **Criticism may come to the leader for four reasons.**

• *Criticism serves as a reminder that we are accountable and responsible for what we say and do.* The word *responsible* means "able to respond" or "to give an answer." Being responsible is a willingness to say, "I have the answer. I said it, and I will stand behind my words."

• *Criticism should humble us as it reminds us of the greatness of our work as Christians and our own personal unworthiness.* A tremendous man who was being criticized about being unworthy to preach and to pastor his church called me for advice.

After I listened to him, I simply asked, "Are you?"

"When you put it that way, Brother Schaap, no, not really," he replied. "Are you worthy to pastor your church?"

"No," I answered. "The critics are right—you are not worthy! No one is truly worthy. Criticism is a reminder that nobody is worthy to preach the unsearchable riches of Christ."

Criticism is a reminder that we are not worthy to be called *Christ ones*—"Christians." Criticism should humble us and show us how unworthy we are. We are just sinners saved by grace.

• *Criticism should convict us of the incredible injustice God receives at the hands and mouths of mankind.* As disappointing and hurtful as criticism is to us, how much more so must it be for a holy and righteous God to receive it? After all, what has God done to deserve any criticism? For the God Who created the heavens and the earth in six days to listen to the pathetic excuses of humanity to demand their rights, threaten to do what they want to do, and refuse to obey Him is incomprehensible!

Criticism reminds me that God never deserves a negative thought. *"From the rising of the sun unto the going down of the same the LORD's name is to be praised."* (Psalm 113:3) And when we don't praise His name, what a high offense that must be to Him! Romans 3:23 says, *"For all have sinned, and come short of the glory of God."* What is the sin that we commit? We fail to give glory to God. This verse means that if we fail to give glory to God, we have committed an egregious sin.

We call those who smoke and drink and curse "sinners," but these sins do not constitute the "great" sin; the great sin is not to give God the glory due Him! But God is patient—even though we do not deserve His patience.

• **Criticism reminds us not only that we are responsible for what we say, but also in many respects, we are accountable for what people think we said.** That statement is painful. Real maturity says, "I am sorry that you misunderstood my words. I apologize because that is not what I intended." A real man (or a real woman) apologizes and properly restates the thought in understandable words and language that properly convey his heart.

5. Criticism teaches us to be exceedingly careful with the reputations and testimonies of one another. The sinful nature of man tends to readily pick up on the criticism of other people and to believe it without any credible documentation. This statement being generally true, let us always be exceedingly circumspect with one another's name and testimony.

We cannot call people on the carpet for the perceived expertise of their critics. That perception is where good people make the mistake of partly believing what might not be true. Documentation, evidence, and validation must be provided. I am continually amazed at the poor research most critics exhibit. Don't be afraid to challenge the integrity of someone's research.

6. Questions concerning what another believer has reportedly said or done should be approached with the demand for Scriptural evidence.

7. If we have sincere questions about another, we must extend the courtesy of personally contacting that one with the concerns. If you think something evil about someone, have the courtesy to contact that person and say, "I heard something that I do not want to believe, and I want to hear the answer from you."

8. Even if the questions are confirmed, we cannot let the cause of Christ take a backseat to our personal concerns.

9. Of the disagreements we have with one another, 99.9 percent should stay strictly between the direct parties involved. Just as in a marriage or in a family, squabbles with other Christians should stay inside the home. Wise couples keep the squabbles inside the integrity of the family unit. In the same way, it is unethical and disrespectful to our Saviour to talk about His children publicly in a negative or disparaging manner. If you have a problem with someone, go straight to that person. That is exactly what the Scripture teaches in Matthew 18.

Someone has said that in order to avoid criticism, one must do nothing, say nothing, be nothing. What a sad way to live life! The unfavorable judgment and disapproval of our fellow men is never easy to endure; however, the one who lives with criticism joins ranks with the greatest Servant Leader who ever lived—Christ. Like Jesus, the servant leader must learn to live above the criticism of others.

"You should do your duty in all things.
You can never do more.
You should never wish to do less."
– General Robert E. Lee

DEVELOPING THE CHARACTER OF CHRIST

"Now before the feast of the passover, when Jesus knew that his hour was come that he should depart out of this world unto the Father, having loved his own which were in the world, he loved them unto the end. And supper being ended, the devil having now put into the heart of Judas Iscariot, Simon's son, to betray him; Jesus knowing that the Father had given all things into his hands, *and that he was come from God, and went to God; He riseth from supper, and laid aside his garments; and took a towel, and girded himself. After that he poureth water into a bason, and began to wash the disciples' feet, and to wipe them with the towel wherewith he was girded. Then cometh he to Simon Peter: and Peter saith unto him, Lord, dost thou wash my feet? Jesus answered and said unto him, What I do thou knowest not now; but thou shalt know here-after. Peter saith unto him, Thou shalt never wash my feet. Jesus answered him, If I wash thee not, thou hast no part with me. Simon Peter saith unto him, Lord, not my feet only, but also my hands and my head. Jesus saith to him, He that is washed needeth not save to wash his feet, but is clean every whit: and ye are clean, but not all. For he knew who should betray him; therefore said he, Ye are not all clean. So after he had washed their feet, and had taken his garments, and was set down again, he said unto them, Know ye what I have done to you? Ye call me Master and Lord: and ye say well; for so I am. If I then, your Lord and Master, have washed your feet; ye also ought to wash one another's feet. For I have given you an example, that ye should do as I have done to you."* (John 13:1-15)

"Leaders of character value the people whom they lead and serve in contrast to leaders without character, who abuse people as a means toward self-serving ends.[1]

The only kind of leader that God validates is a servant leader. In a sense servant leadership is demonstrating the character of God or the character of Christ. It is leadership that understands it has more of a duty than simply to be in charge of something. It is a position that has accepted the challenge of taking the people not just to a position or a place, but to a character.

God says a leader is someone who has established the character of Christ and is taking the people under his leadership toward developing that character. Character is a characteristic or a trait that identifies you with the one for whom the trait is named. Working to develop the character of Christ means we want to develop traits in our life that remind other people who know Christ that we emulate or copy Him.

To develop character in another requires you first to be a servant. However, it is impossible for man to assimilate the right kind of Christlike character because Christ's character was epitomized by His making Himself of no reputation, humbling Himself, and emptying Himself. Copying the character of Christ begins with a person's willingness to say, "I will empty myself of everything that does not reflect Christ so I can fill myself with everything that is Christ. In doing so, I can be used to develop that kind of character in my followers."

In the world's model of leadership, people can be taught many leadership principles. They can be taken to war and win that war. They can be taken into the business realm and be taught how to win the battle of cornering the market in a certain area and becoming the number-one business in that area. However, these examples have precious little to do with developing the character of Christ.

Over half of John chapter 13 deals with 7 days in the 33½ year life of Jesus Christ. Basically, John 13 focuses on that last week of Jesus' life and, in particular, addresses the last three days before the Crucifixion. Jesus is having the last meal He will ever eat on earth.

He is teaching His men about leadership because He is mere hours away from having those men demonstrate one more time that they didn't "catch" what He was teaching. But He knows they are just about to catch it, and He is sharing His last little nuggets of wisdom. He knows they have focused on being a part of the kingdom, sitting beside Him in the kingdom, and ruling with Him in the kingdom. He knew He had to get them away from that mentality, or Christianity would die.

In developing the character of Christ, a leader must ask himself an important question: can God trust me?

- **Can God trust me with knowledge?**

Can God trust me with knowing information about other people? Knowing the weaknesses and failures about people implies a contract of trust. When God calls a man into the ministry, he will find out both the worst and the best of people. A man of God must learn to keep confidences.

Not one of the other 11 disciples knew about Judas from the mouth of Jesus until the moment that Judas was sent on his assignment. When John asked which one of the disciples would betray Him, Jesus said, "It is the one to whom I gave some food." Jesus did not give a huge hint because all of them had been eating.

- **Can God trust me with unstable followers or co-workers?**

God's trusting me means I will not hurt these co-workers; rather, I will be willing to humble myself before them.

- ***Can God trust me to serve without prejudice?***

The word *prejudice* means "to pre-judge." Can God trust me to serve without my passing judgment on others and stating, "I don't think I like that person, so he will not receive the benefit of my service." Jesus offered this truth when He was kneeling and washing the feet of His disciples. God wants His leaders to serve **all** of His children.

- ***Can God trust me to set an example?***

Can God trust me to understand that there is a greater cause than even the personal hurt I will suffer at the hands of people who don't understand servant leadership?

DEVELOPING THE CHARACTER OF CHRIST

1. Leadership is all about trust. *"Now before the feast of the passover, when Jesus knew that his hour was come that he should depart out of this world unto the Father, having loved his own which were in the world, he loved them unto the end. And supper being ended, the devil having now put into the heart of Judas Iscariot, Simon's son, to betray him; Jesus knowing that the Father had given all things into his hands, and that he was come from God, and went to God."* (John 13:1-3)

I do not believe that as a little infant Jesus knew He was the Son of God. The Bible says He grew in knowledge, in stature, and in favor with God and man. As Jesus is growing up, He comes into the understanding of Who He is. By the time He is 12 years of age, He possesses a very good grasp that He is the Father's Son. He is already aware that He has a mission to accomplish that far surpasses pounding nails in wood and being a carpenter's son. No doubt Jesus understands that the God about Whom He has been reading in synagogue school really is the God He knows.

When He reads *"...he hath no form nor comeliness; and when we shall see him, there is no beauty that we should desire him,"* in Isaiah 53:2 and then reads *"But he was wounded for our transgressions, he was bruised for our iniquities: the chastisement of our peace was upon him; and with his stripes we are healed,"* Jesus must have known that Scripture was also referring to Him because He was full of the knowledge of the Holy Ghost.

I wonder if He ever read Psalm 22 which says that His hands and feet were pierced. I wonder if His feet and hands ever twinged in anticipation of what the Holy Ghost inside of Him surely knew for certain would inevitably happen because the Holy Ghost had penned those words. There never was a moment that Jesus Christ was not filled with the Holy Ghost. No doubt His understanding became stronger and stronger as He grew into the understanding that "God is My Father; My Father is my God. God and I are Father and Son."

And one of the wonderful truths that Jesus grasped was that God Almighty trusted Him! As Jesus read the Book that He had written and began to comprehend it in a way that nobody else comprehended it, He began to understand that He was reading about the trust factor between the Father and the Son. He began to understand fully that He was part of that wonderful plan of redemption, and He understood that His Father trusted Him with this knowledge.

An understanding must come in the heart of every parent, every Sunday school teacher, and every leader—whether in the secular arena or in a spiritual position—that God has placed them in a position of leadership because He trusts them. He trusts us with the knowledge of what we will learn as well as the knowledge of what we have been given. What is missing so much in leadership is the ability to understand that God believes in us.

Does God trust you? Can God trust you with the weaknesses of people? God says leadership is a matter of trust.

2. Trust is all about love. Jesus understood that His Father loved Him. John 13:3 says, *"Jesus knowing that the Father had given all things into his hands."* Love and trust cannot be separated.

3. A servant leader must know that all that he has was given to him from the Father. Do not jockey for position—because you do not want to be given a leadership position you have not earned. You do not want to be in charge of anything knowing that you connived to have it. Know that the position you have was thrust upon you by Almighty God without the manipulation of any human handcraft.

4. A servant leader must know that he was chosen or sent by God and therefore must answer to God. Having this knowledge gives a servant leader the boldness and the courage he has because there is no other place to find courage. "Courage is not the absence of fear but rather the presence of resolve and determination."[2] The only real power that a servant leader has comes when he knows that someday he will personally stand before Jesus Christ and answer for how his people listened to him, how they responded to him, how often they came to hear him, and how they accepted and utilized what was given to them.

That knowledge is what gave Dr. Jack Hyles that edge in his voice and the dynamics in his speech. He knew he had a day of reckoning with God and that God would look at him and say, "Jack Hyles, would you please explain to Me thus and so while you were in charge of that church?" A servant leader knows he answers only to God because God gave the servant leader his job and God holds him responsible.

5. **The servant leader must know and understand the greater purpose or calling of God.** John 13:5 says, *"After that he poureth water into a bason, and began to wash the disciples' feet, and to wipe them with the towel wherewith he was girded."* The worthiness of the worker is not always the issue. Jesus washed the feet of Simon Peter, knowing Simon would deny Him. He also washed the feet of James, the other Simon, Thaddaeus, Nathaniel, and Andrew, who would all leave Him. He even washed the feet of Judas, who would betray Him! Jesus gave every Christian an example of servanthood by washing the feet of His disciples and then charging us to do likewise. Jesus knew a servant leader does not look at the worthiness of the person because some of the greatest works of God are performed by some unworthy people. After all, Moses was a murderer; Abraham was a two-faced liar who committed adultery; and David was guilty of the horrible, egregious sin of adultery. The list goes on and on.

God will judge us according to our works—not necessarily our worthiness. The Bible says that when a Christian stands before Jesus Christ, he will have hay, wood, and stubble or gold, silver, and precious stones. God will examine his works—not his worthiness—because if He examined one's worthiness, it would doubtless all be wood, hay, and stubble.

Goodness and worthiness are found in the works we do. Certainly we are all unworthy. Thankfully, God says the person who produces the work is worthy of Him. God has a name for a person who will not work—wicked and slothful servant.

If the Son of God was worthy of humbling Himself to wash the feet of a traitor, then we are also worthy of the work and of the humility.

6. **Servant leadership is centered in humility.** If a critic is soul winning and church building, leave him alone! Some critical people are used by God to do the work of God. I leave anyone who criticizes me alone if he is soul winning and building a work of God. Why? Because it is not important whether I am worthy or unworthy of criticism or whether that person is worthy or unworthy to criticize. If he is doing the work of God, I am to leave him alone! Not one of the disciples thought Judas was a slouch. All of his co-workers thought he was doing the work of God as well as the next man. Too many men of God forget the work of God as they defend themselves.

7. **The veil between the physical and the spiritual is very thin in a true servant leader.** *"Peter saith unto him, Thou shalt never wash my feet. Jesus answered him, If I wash thee not, thou hast no part with me. Simon Peter saith unto him, Lord, not*

my feet only, but also my hands and my head. Jesus saith to him, He that is washed needeth not save to wash his feet, but is clean every whit: and ye are clean, but not all." (John 13:8-10) Jesus lived with His hands so much on the heart of His Father, feeling the pulse of God, that I am sure He enjoyed life. I believe He was incredibly aware of the bigness of every situation that came into His life. No doubt, all of life was big to Him.

Jesus turned every conversation into a spiritual question because that veil was so thin. When He asked the Samaritan woman at the well for water because He was thirsty, she was surprised that He would ask her, a Samaritan, to draw water for Him—a Jew. If He were talking today, He might have said, "Ma'am, if you knew Who was asking you to give water, you would ask Me for water everlasting. I would give it to you, and you would never thirst again."

As a servant leader, Jesus looked for every opportunity He could to teach a truth, mentor, and train because He knew His time was limited. He knew the whole of the kingdom would rest in the hands of His disciples. He desperately wanted them to catch the philosophy of servant leadership.

Christianity is fast losing ground because those of us who pretend to be leaders do not keep our hand on the pulse of God. The whole business of servant leadership isn't about a position or possessions. Christians need to take off the jacket, bow the knee, show humility, learn the character of God, and serve others—no matter how worthy or unworthy the person is—because God's work is worthy of someone who understands the principle of servant leadership. "To lead is to serve."[3]

> "Servant leadership is not just another management
> technique. It is a way of life for those
> with servant hearts."
> – Ken Blanchard

THE SPIRIT OF SERVANT LEADERSHIP

"Then Moses heard the people weep throughout their families, every man in the door of his tent: and the anger of the LORD was kindled greatly; Moses also was displeased. And Moses said unto the LORD, Wherefore hast thou afflicted thy servant? and wherefore have I not found favour in thy sight, that thou layest the burden of all this people upon me? Have I conceived all this people? have I begotten them, that thou shouldest say unto me, Carry them in thy

*bosom, as a nursing father beareth the sucking child, unto the land
which thou swarest unto their fathers? Whence should I have flesh
to give unto all this people? for they weep unto me, saying, Give us
flesh, that we may eat. I am not able to bear all this people alone,
because it is too heavy for me. And if thou deal thus with me, kill
me, I pray thee, out of hand, if I have found favour in thy sight; and
let me not see my wretchedness."* (Numbers 11:10-15)

In Numbers 11 Moses was experiencing an extremely difficult time in his ministry. In his feeling of being overwhelmed
as the leader of the children of Israel, he begged for God's help
in understanding his situation. He said, "You have to help me,
God; I have had about all I can take with Your children's whin-
ing, complaining, and playing the 'blame' game." Moses told
God he desperately needed His guidance and help in leading
the people.

Moses was the greatest leader in the Old Testament.
How would you like to relocate one and a half million
complaining people? It was hard...and tiring. And as his
nation grew, Moses became more tired, and the people's
needs went unmet. The problem? Moses was trying to do
it all himself.[1]

Numbers 11:25-30 gives God's answer to Moses' very
transparent words of despair. *"And the LORD came down in a
cloud, and spake unto him, and **took of the spirit that was upon
him,** and gave it unto the seventy elders: and it came to pass, that,
when the spirit rested upon them, they prophesied, and did not*

cease. But there remained two of the men in the camp, the name of the one was Eldad, and the name of the other Medad: and the spirit rested upon them; and they were of them that were written, but went not out unto the tabernacle: and they prophesied in the camp. And there ran a young man, and told Moses, and said, Eldad and Medad do prophesy in the camp. And Joshua the son of Nun, the servant of Moses, one of his young men, answered and said, My lord Moses, forbid them. And Moses said unto him, Enviest thou for my sake? would God that all the LORD's people were prophets, and that the LORD would put his spirit upon them! And Moses gat him into the camp, he and the elders of Israel." God's answer for Moses' dilemma was for Moses to personally choose 70 men who felt like Moses did, saw situations the way he saw them, and comprehended the way Moses led. According to verse 25, God then took of the spirit that was upon Moses and placed it upon these chosen 70 elders. These men, in turn, would remove some of the incredible pressures Moses faced every day.

A similar type of story regarding the spirit of a leader is given in II Kings 2:9, *"And it came to pass, when they were gone over, that Elijah said unto Elisha, Ask what I shall do for thee, before I be taken away from thee. And Elisha said, I pray thee, let a double portion of thy spirit be upon me."* Though this story in II Kings 2 is somewhat different from the story of Moses, what Elisha had noticed about Elijah was his spirit.

From these two Biblical illustrations, we can surmise that one of the greatest attributes of a servant leader is his spirit. In fact, I believe the standout characteristic of a true servant leader is his spirit. In this chapter I want to address the spirit of a servant leader, and truthfully, we will barely scratch the surface on the topic. Not only did Moses and Elijah possess the spirit of a servant leader, but that standout spirit also characterized the life of Daniel. *"Then this Daniel was preferred above the presidents and princes, because an excellent spirit was in him; and the king thought to set him over the whole realm."* (Daniel 6:3)

Moses, Elijah, Elisha, and Daniel worked amazing miracles. Though Moses performed ten incredible miracles in the land of Egypt, God did not give the 70 men power to perform miracles; He gave them something else. Elijah performed a number of miracles, and Elisha performed exactly twice as many miracles, but Elisha didn't ask for miracle power; he wanted Elijah's spirit on him. Daniel performed amazing miracles, interpreted extraordinary visions, outlined the course of Israeli history for hundreds of years to come, and prophesied the coming of Jesus Christ. However, that wasn't the standout statement made about Daniel. What was standout about Daniel was his excellent spirit. As I study the lives of these men, I believe they exemplified true servant leadership.

1. The spirit of the servant leader attracts followers. Many impressive, talented people do amazing feats, but as a rule, we do not follow those people; we enjoy their talents. For instance, we might enjoy a preacher's preaching, a musician's music, a comedian's humor, or an actor's ability to depict a certain character, but enjoying that talent does not mean we will follow that person. What causes people to want to follow someone is his excellent spirit. Through the years I have had the privilege of personally knowing some phenomenal pastors who weren't the best of preachers but who have built some great churches, but each possessed an excellent spirit. They captured my heart with that spirit.

I am thinking of a church that had several thousand members, and I had the privilege of knowing the pastor quite well. By his own admission he said, "I can't preach very well." And truthfully, whenever he made this statement, I wanted to say, "I know." He truly wasn't a very good preacher, but he had an excellent spirit, and all of his people were captured by the incredible spirit he possessed.

My predecessor, Dr. Jack Hyles, was a multi-talented man; single-talented men do not build ministries like the ministry Brother Hyles built. I believe Dr. Hyles' standout characteristic was not his preaching, and many people would probably disagree with me on that particular observation. I do not believe the standout characteristic about Brother Hyles was his incredible gift for administration, though he surely possessed that ability. I believe the standout quality about Brother Hyles was his spirit.

His presence would lighten up a room—not just because he had a bigger-than-life spirit or personality. He worked at making people feel better for his having crossed their path. He made it a personal challenge to bring cheer to every person he met. His magnanimous spirit magnetically attracted people, and then he showed them an even bigger spirit than a man normally had. People were captivated by his ability to show forth a right spirit, and that spirit is what always attracts followers to a leader.

Irwin Federman, the president and CEO of Monolithic Memories, one of the most successful of the high-tech companies in the Silicon Valley, addresses the leader-follower relationship:

> If you think about it, people love others not for who they are, but for how they make us feel. We willingly follow others for much the same reason. It makes us feel good to do so. Now, we also follow platoon sergeants, self-centered geniuses, demanding spouses, bosses of various persuasions and others for a variety of reasons as well. But none of those reasons involves the person's leadership qualities. In order to **willingly** accept the direction of another individual, it must feel good to do so. This business of making another person feel good in the unspectacular course of his daily comings and goings is, in my view, the very essence of leadership.[2]

Dr. Jack Hyles made it his business to make every person he met feel better for having crossed his path.

The servant leader, Jesus Christ, performed many miracles, and certainly people followed Him because of those miracles. However, His 12 men who followed Him, followed Him because of His spirit—not the miracles He worked. When Jesus told them He would be leaving, He told them He would not leave them comfortless or spiritless; He would give them something better than His being on earth Himself. He was going to give them His spirit. That spirit of Christ draws people, and the spirit of a leader draws followers.

Several years ago Dr. Hyles asked me to go to a church to observe a good man whose church was seemingly dying. He explained that his schedule was booked in advance for three or four years in the future, and he was afraid that the church would die before he could meet with the man. I did as he requested and went to observe the ministry. I arrived on a Saturday afternoon, spent time with the family Saturday evening, and attended church on Sunday morning. I told the pastor I was there only to observe.

On Monday morning, I met with the pastor. By that time, I had compiled about a page and a half of simple, practical recommendations, so I shared them with him. "This is very helpful, Dr. Schaap," he commented, "but what is your personal opinion?"

"I don't mean to be negative or ugly," I started, "but my personal opinion is your spirit stinks! You are doing everything in your power to drive away people! Even as you greeted people, I felt like you were holding a big banner that said, 'Sinners not welcome.' You were gruff with people. You greeted one lady visitor wearing trousers, 'Ma'am, you may come this week dressed like you are, but don't come dressed like that to the house of God next week.' In the pulpit, my brother, you scolded the people who came! Why?"

"You know, you are right," he admitted. "I was yelling at them about the people who were not there."

"Don't yell at the people who come because of the people

who don't come," I said. "They are the good guys! We need to discuss your spirit." Max DuPree made a singular, but obvious, statement in his book, *Leadership Is an Art,* "Without people, there is no need for leaders."[3] This good man was well on his way to having an empty church! I spent the whole day with him, and I shared about 25 ideas to help his spirit. That church started growing; in fact, it skyrocketed in attendance! He wrote to me and shared that the offerings were better and the people had a much better spirit. That good man learned the important lesson that people are not necessarily drawn by a man of God's preaching or by his amazing Sunday school skills. People are drawn by the spirit of a leader.

I remember teaching in Sunday school holding two babies in my arms because they would only be quiet if I held them. Two young girls had brought their babies to class, and when they would not be quiet, I said, "Let me hold them." People who came to the class said, "I am glad I go to a class where we are accepted and loved!" I was not there for myself; I was there for the people! A class that grows and thrives is not growing because one teaches or preaches or organizes any better than another, but because he brings an added spirit. That spirit is what people like to follow. A good spirit creates a following.

THE SPIRIT OF A SERVANT LEADER

1. **The spirit of a servant leader is not dominated by circumstances, nor is it mercurial or unpredictable.** Servant leadership starts with an excellent spirit, and when the leader

possesses that spirit, he will draw a good measure of followers. Followers are not encouraged by a leader who is depressed. "When you become a leader, you lose the right to think about yourself."[4] People are encouraged by a leader who, in spite of what he is facing, fights himself and is on the winning side. A happy, positive, excellent spirit rallies people.

When I grew up as a boy, I grew up in a home that was a place where people liked to visit. I knew when my wife and I were married that I wanted to build the same kind of home. My wife-to-be asked me, "How do you describe the kind of home you want us to build?"

"Happy," I answered. "I would like to build a happy home with Christ as the head of it."

Like the home I enjoyed as a boy, our house soon became the hangout place for our neighborhood. I remember one time when we had over 40 neighborhood children sitting on the porch at our house. Kenny was just a little tyke, but he led them in singing. Jaclynn then stood and preached a sermon just like she had seen it preached in church. All those kids wanted to be saved. As I was watching through the picture window, they started marching single file singing, "I'm going on a soul hunt, I'm not ashamed, Jesus in my heart and the Bible in my hand." They marched up and down the neighborhood singing that song!

When those neighbor kids came to our house, anything edible was soon gone. Home was where they wanted to be, but why our home? Only one reason! It was happy! A good spirit reigned there. A mother lived there who enjoyed kids. A dad and a mom lived there who loved each other. When I came home and saw the kids watching, I grabbed my wife, hugged her and kissed her, and all my spectators said, "Oooooh!" They were all watching and enjoying the love displayed in our home. Kids would say to our children, "Boy, I wish your dad was my dad," or "I wish your mom and dad were my parents."

Their statements would break my heart, but I always thought, that attitude is what I want for the kids—a happy spirit. I want them to think this home is the greatest place in the world to be.

None of the neighborhood kids came in and said, "Oh, Dr. Schaap, thou teachest the Bible with such great execution and deliverance." Those kids didn't care a thing about preaching. They cared about how happy we were. They cared about how even-tempered we were. Peace, happiness, harmony, and laughter reigned in our home.

A happy spirit drew us to Brother Hyles, and that spirit is also what we liked about the great men whom Brother Hyles brought as guests to First Baptist Church. He knew what drew and attracted followers.

2. The spirit of a servant leader is a spirit that others want to copy. When Elijah was about to go Home to Heaven, "*...Elijah said unto Elisha, Ask what I shall do for thee, before I be taken away from thee....*" (II Kings 2:9) Elisha didn't say, "Teach me how you call fire down from Heaven; I want to burn up some prophets like you did!"

"*...And Elisha said, I pray thee, let a double portion of thy spirit be upon me.*" No wonder Elijah said, "*...Thou hast asked* *a hard thing…."* (II Kings 2:10) A leader who possesses a good spirit soon discovers the hardest thing to maintain is a good spirit because everything in the world tries to make him have a foul spirit.

After pastoring for almost seven years in First Baptist Church of Hammond, Indiana, I marvel that Brother Hyles ever smiled at all. The pressure he endured is just unbelievable with the correspondence demands, the continuous lists of phone calls that need to be answered, the counseling sessions, and the day-to-day problems that constantly arise.

I still have many people ask, "Brother Schaap, how did Dr. Hyles maintain that top-of-the-morning feeling all the time?" Truly, I cannot say he always was on top, but I can say that he always possessed the right kind of spirit. Evidently Elisha thought the same about Elijah. Evidently Joshua and those 70 elders thought the same of Moses. Evidently the unsaved rulers who worked with Daniel thought the same about Daniel. Great leaders possess an excellent, well-disciplined spirit.

A happy spirit is what people want to copy. Wouldn't you love to always be as happy as Brother Hyles was? Wouldn't you always love to be as upbeat and positive as the people whom you admire? Truthfully, much of a person's happy spirit might very well be the result of discipline. The servant leader who wants to follow the Biblical model of leadership must learn what people want to copy from him.

3. The spirit of a servant leader is a whole or complete spirit through which the Holy Spirit is able to work. The spirit of the servant leader allows God to work in him. I Thessalonians 5 contains a powerful paragraph of teaching that every servant leader should memorize. Verse 19 says, *"Quench not the Spirit."* *Spirit* in this passage refers to the Holy Spirit—God's Spirit. God wants to work in a person's life without being quenched. He can work in the life of a believer if that believer is willing to develop the arena through which He can do His work. The following are six ways the Holy Spirit can work in a person without being quenched or extinguished.

- *"Rejoice evermore."* Every Christian must have an attitude of joy and continual praise on his lips.
- *"Pray without ceasing."* Don't ever give up on prayer. How long has it been since you poured out your heart to God? Prayer is a language that God understands. In his book *The Prayer Life*, Andrew Murray wrote,

Little of the Word with little prayer is death to the spiritual life. Much of the Word with little prayer gives a sickly life. Much prayer with little of the Word gives more life, but without stedfastness. A full measure of the Word and prayer each day gives a healthy and powerful life.[5]

God's Spirit works through praying Christians.

- *"In every thing give thanks...."* God loves a person with a happy, grateful tongue.
- *"Despise not prophesyings."* God loves preaching, and He wants His people to love preaching.
- *"Prove all things; hold fast that which is good."* Choose what you believe and don't change. Don't always be

testing the waters, changing Bible versions, changing churches, and changing ideas. God wants His people to be anchored to a rock.

- *"Abstain from all appearance of evil."* Christians should be aware of Satan's tricks and the masks he wears and recognize him for who he is.

A servant leader who consistently rejoices, prays, gives thanks, enjoys the preaching of God's Word, proves all things, holds fast to the good, and abstains from the appearance of evil makes a complete Christian—one through whom the Spirit of God can work. The spirit of the leader attracts the followers. Likewise, the spirit of the follower affects the spirit of the leader. The spirit of the servant leader is what people want to copy.

TEN SPIRITS FROM PROVERBS

1. A Faithful Spirit. Proverbs 11:13 says, *"A talebearer revealeth secrets: but he that is of a faithful spirit concealeth the matter."* The ability to keep a secret is a faithful spirit. This trusted person knows information that could hurt someone else, but he has the needed discipline never to tell anyone the matter. This leader would never share a negative report.

2. A Hasty Spirit. Proverbs 14:29 says, *"He that is slow to wrath is of great understanding: but he that is hasty of spirit exalteth folly."* The word *wrath* means "venting." Anger is an emotion; wrath is an expression. Wrath is the venting of anger. The Bible says that a hasty spirit is one that vents in an angry way. "Venting can actually serve to prolong anger and may also make it easier to get angry again in the future because you have solidified your beliefs."[6] A leader cannot afford to be quick to speak angrily or be quick in venting his emotions.

3.   A Perverse Spirit. Proverbs 15:4 says, *"A wholesome tongue is a tree of life: but perverseness therein is a breach in the spirit."* The Bible describes the perverse spirit as a spirit that twists or distorts a fact. Too many very good people are not trustworthy with facts. They would probably never tell a bad story or expose a secret, but they never are careful with the details of a story. They are reckless with the facts and information.

4.   A Broken Spirit. Proverbs 15:13 says, *"A merry heart maketh a cheerful countenance: but by sorrow of the heart the spirit is broken."* A broken spirit is manifested in two ways: a sad heart and an ugly countenance. One's countenance is the mirror of his spirit. Some people feel that it is pious to look sad. No! Looking sad looks ugly. The time and the place to be burdened is during time spent alone with God.

God says if we do have a sorrowful heart, we're not to let anyone know about it. Too many people in Christianity are sad. In my mind, sadness and Christianity shouldn't really go together. Nothing is wrong with being depressed or sad, but I just don't think we should show it.

5.   A Haughty Spirit. Proverbs 16:18 says, *"Pride goeth before destruction, and an haughty spirit before a fall."* A haughty spirit is a proud, arrogant spirit. Arrogant people seem always to talk about themselves, what they have done, and what they are accomplishing. In their arrogance, they try to remind others that they are superior. Nobody wants to copy that kind of spirit.

So many talented people have an arrogant, haughty spirit. I am reminded of the time I went to the Western Golf Open about 15 years ago. Someone bought tickets for my dad, my son, and me to go. It was the chance of a lifetime, and at the time, I knew most of the names of the golfers who were playing. I maneuvered into a position where I could see some of the big name players. My dad said, "You want to get some autographs?"

I said, "Sure, I would like that." We were standing at a place where I could have blocked them if I had put out my arm. I said to one person, "Hey, can I get your autograph?"

"Oh, sure," he said. He took out a pen and signed.

The big name player—the one we were all waiting for—had made a bad putt, and when he was asked for an autograph, he retorted, "Leave me alone!"

My dad said, "Isn't that amazing! All bent out of shape because he missed a little putt. I know it is his job, but we are paying the money. What an ugly, arrogant attitude!"

Nobody said to that man, "I would like to be just like you someday!"

On the other hand, the reason Arnold Palmer had an army following him was that Arnie had a very upbeat spirit. He entertained the spectators while he was playing. People enjoy being with someone who doesn't take himself too seriously.

6. A Humble Spirit. Proverbs 16:19 says, *"Better it is to be of an humble spirit with the lowly, than to divide the spoil with the proud."* The word *humble* is derived from the word *humus* meaning "soil." A humble man understands his roots—from where he came. "People with humility don't think less of themselves; they just think about themselves less."[7]

7. A Disciplined Spirit. Proverbs 16:32 says, *"He that is slow to anger is better than the mighty; and he that ruleth his spirit than he that taketh a city."* A disciplined spirit is a controlled spirit, and a disciplined spirit always starts with the tongue. The man who can control his tongue possesses a great spirit.

8. An Excellent Spirit. Proverbs 17:27, *"He that hath knowledge spareth his words: and a man of understanding is of an excellent spirit."* The person who has an excellent spirit restrains his words.

9. A Wounded Spirit. Proverbs 18:14 says, *"The spirit of a man will sustain his infirmity; but a wounded spirit who can bear?"* The word *wounded* means "worn down, unable to lift yourself up when you are down." A happy-spirited person is someone who has discovered how to pick himself up when nobody else can or when nobody else wants to or when everyone else is trying to push him down. This person finds a way to come out on top in spite of his circumstances—when no one else expected him to be there.

Dr. Jack Hyles personified the definition of the happy-spirited person—he truly lived above the clouds. During some very depressing days, he somehow found a way to come out to the pulpit. King David encouraged himself in the Lord, and that is why he was the king.

10. An Undefended Spirit. Proverbs 25:28, *"He that hath no rule over his own spirit is like a city that is broken down, and without walls."* I also call the undefended spirit the unserviced spirit because the Bible wording in the Hebrew means "a spirit that is not maintained." Just like a car needs regular servicing, a man's spirit also needs to be maintained.

One's spirit can be likened to a brand-new, shiny vehicle. To keep that vehicle "happy," it needs to be washed and vacuumed weekly; the trash needs to be removed on a daily basis; and periodically the clutter should be cleaned from the glove box, the center console, and the dashboard. If the oil light comes on and the brakes squeal, the car is not disposed of; it is taken to a station for servicing.

Likewise, the servant leader Christian needs to work on servicing his spirit in the same way. The spirit responds to listening to good music, talking with God, rejoicing evermore, praying without ceasing, and giving thanks in everything. The servant leader must keep his spirit serviced!

> "…above all a leader must be genuine—
> his own true self, not an imitation of some other,
> be that other ever so successful."
> – Lincoln Andrews

THE INSECURITY OF THE SERVANT LEADER

"And he came to Capernaum: and being in the house he asked them, What was it that ye disputed among yourselves by the way? But they held their peace: for by the way they had disputed among themselves, who should be the greatest. And he sat down, and called the twelve, and saith unto them, If any man desire to be first, the same shall be last of all, and servant of all. And he took a child, and set him in the midst of them: and when he had taken him in his *arms, he said unto them, Whosoever shall receive one of such children in my name, receiveth me: and whosoever shall receive me, receiveth not me, but him that sent me. And John answered him, saying, Master, we saw one casting out devils in thy name, and he followeth not us: and we forbad him, because he followeth not us. But Jesus said, Forbid him not: for there is no man which shall do a miracle in my name, that can lightly speak evil of me. For he that is not against us is on our part. For whosoever shall give you a cup of water to drink in my name, because ye belong to Christ, verily I say unto you, he shall not lose his reward."* (Mark 9:33-41)

Parallel Passages: Luke 9:49-50; Matthew 20

James and John, two culprits in the "insecurity department," campaign throughout the Scriptures to make sure everyone is lined up behind them, doing exactly what they decide is proper for everyone else to do. For instance, James and John forbade someone from doing a work because they did not feel he was a part of "their" team. They informed this man he had to change what he was doing.

In Matthew 20 James' and John's mother makes a special request of Jesus on behalf of her sons. She asks for them to sit on either side of Jesus when He rules in the kingdom. Matthew 20:20-22 illustrates the true price of being a servant leader. *"Then came to him the mother of Zebedee's children with her sons, worshipping him, and desiring a certain thing of him. And he said unto her, What wilt thou? She saith unto him, Grant that these my two sons may sit, the one on thy right hand, and the other on the left, in thy kingdom. But Jesus answered and said, Ye know not what ye ask. Are ye able to drink of the cup that I shall drink of, and to be baptized with the baptism that I am baptized with? They say unto him, We are able."*

James and John had no idea what they were asking of their Saviour! In a sense Jesus reprimanded their mother and told her that seeking position isn't what they were to worry about on this earth. He told her it was not His business nor His mission on earth to worry about who would sit by Him in the kingdom. His Father in Heaven had already decided who would be worthy of that position.

As James and John jockeyed for position, even to enlisting the aid of their mother, their lives were not characterized by servant leadership. At this point in their ministry, James and John had not the slightest idea about servant leadership. They were focused on being in charge.

These men believed they were close to Jesus, but other than the Apostle Paul, no one in the Bible appears to be closer emotionally to Jesus Christ than John. Other than the Apostle Paul, no other man writes more about the love of God. Of course, the Apostle Paul wrote 14 books in the New Testament, and by the sheer volume of Paul's writings, of necessity, he receives the award for writing the most about the love of God. Still, John is known as the Apostle of love, whereas Peter is called the Apostle of hope, and Paul is called the Apostle of salvation, redemption, and justification.

John wrote a total of five books—the Gospel of John; I, II,

and III John; and Revelation. John suffered much for the cause of Jesus Christ. He was taken prisoner, survived being totally immersed in a vat of boiling oil, left horribly disfigured, and was then exiled to suffer on the isle of Patmos. There on Patmos he saw the visions of Revelation and was used mightily of God to record them. John was truly an amazing man!

As the disciple whom Jesus loved, John, as well as his brother James, writes more about the love relationship between God and man.

"Who are you, John?"

"I am the disciple whom Jesus loves" was the way he described himself. A very humble man, John was very aware and overwhelmed humanly speaking by God's love for him. John was very affectionate and emotional; he was the disciple who laid his head on Jesus' breast. In Bible times, people didn't sit in chairs at tables when they ate; they reclined on a low pallet and leaned on an elbow toward a table. John was seated next to Jesus Christ, and as he talked to the Master, he leaned back to rest his head against Jesus' chest. John was close enough, trusted enough, and intimate enough to be that personal with Jesus Christ. John was enraptured with the love of God and very tuned in to the fiber and being of Jesus. But he was also the one who was most worried about where he fit in.

John and his brother James had the most difficult time accepting their appropriate position of leadership and followship. Their concern over their position brought them great insecurity.

1.   **Those who are most attracted to the love of God**

often need emotional security the most. Sometimes it is incredibly difficult to be a servant leader because of the emotional rejection or lack of protection one has felt in his life. In my counseling and working with Christians, I always find that all people are not drawn to Christianity for the same reasons. Many people are drawn to Christianity by the love of God. Some great men in leadership positions have been very drawn to the cause of Christ by the fact that God loves them. One such man who was very overwhelmed by the love of God was Dr. Jack Hyles. He grew up in a single-parent home without the affection of a father, and on top of that, he was twice rejected by his father—first as a young boy and then when he was called into the ministry. He was a rejected man, and often the most rejected people and the most emotionally insecure people are very drawn to the love of God.

Brother Hyles often quoted poetry about the love of God, wrote poetry about the love of God, and preached sermon series about the love of God. In his book *Meet the Holy Spirit,* Dr. Hyles wrote an in-depth chapter on "Prayer and Love," in which he penned an answer to a preacher's question, "How does your fire stay burning?"

> I immediately replied, "The act of love. It is the setting aside of some time each day during which you think your way into the lives of others."
>
> What is love? God is love. Love is that indefinable word, that indescribable scene, that unfathomable depth, that unreachable height, that unknowable fact; yet, all the

orators with their eloquence, all the artists with their brushes, all the sculptors with their chisels, and all the writers with their quills have not been able to describe love! As was written once on the wall of an insane asylum:

> Could we with ink the ocean fill,
> And were the sky of parchment made,
> Were every stalk on earth a quill,
> And every man a scribe by trade;
> To write the love of God above
> Would drain the ocean dry;
> Nor could the scroll contain the whole,
> Through stretched from sky to sky.

Maybe that person with his mind temporarily ill was saner than all of us, and maybe he understood more about love than the scholars. Whatever love is, when God's children know it, it is the key that unlocks the coffers of glory and propels the generosity of God to send needs and wants to His children which they have requisitioned of Him![1]

Dr. Hyles was very drawn to Jesus because he found in Jesus Christ this incredible God-man Who never rejected him. Emotionally insecure people are drawn to strong, powerful figures who will not reject them and who will offer protection.

I am also overwhelmed by the love of God, but I must admit that the love of God is not what captured my heart and brought me into the ministry. For me, what brought me into the ministry is the incredible work that God wanted done. I am a fairly emotionally secure person, and because of that security, I marvel at the love of God, and I am overwhelmed by the love of God, but I believe I emphasize His grace and His mercy far more as the amazing manner in which God bestows love to us. Truthfully, love is a bit of a mystery to me. I know that God is infinite love, and that concept boggles my mind.

I do, however, understand work. I do understand taking the Gospel to the entire world. That language of work challenges me. Just these two examples illustrate the fact that different people are motivated or drawn to God for different reasons. None of these reasons is either right or wrong; one is not better than another.

Mary Magdalene was drawn to Jesus Christ for one great reason—forgiveness. She was overwhelmed with the knowledge that Someone could forgive her sins. Blind Bartimaeus was drawn to Jesus Christ because his eyesight was restored. Everyone needs a miracle at some time or another; Jesus is a miracle worker. These emotions within the servant leader and within the framework of the world's type of leadership explain why it is so difficult at times to become a servant leader.

2. The more insecure one is, the more difficulty he has with other independent, confident leaders. Twice John accused others of not following Jesus. Insecure people who follow their leader because they need security and protection feel very threatened by someone who does not seem to conform within the framework of what they think every follower should be. Someone off on his own, doing his own thing, or not doing it quite like the textbook will be perceived as a threat. If that leader is doing great works in Jesus' name but he is not on the same team, insecurity begins questioning and says, "How do I know that I am really being used of God? Maybe I am deceived. Maybe I am not involved with the right people. Maybe I haven't found the right leader."

We must keep in mind that Jesus was the only Man Who has ever lived Who is 100% emotionally secure. Jesus was not insecure, nor worried, nor overly confident; He was just very content with Who He was. He was therefore free to work on helping other people get to where they needed to be.

Jesus told John that if a leader was doing something in His name and was not against Him, then that leader was for Him. Jesus was not bothered at all by the security of another leader, but that security sometimes bothers other insecure people.

3. Much of the criticism made toward others in Christianity, including criticism from one leader against another leader, is insecurity's trying to protect his position and influence. One who desires to be secure in his position and calling with Christ should not worry about someone else who is also being used of God. I am a great believer in controlling only that which I have authority to control.

God gave me a profound calling 33 years ago, and that profound calling of God gave me a great sense of security that God can use anyone He wants to use and in whatever way He wants to use them. Some people who are a little insecure often become critical when they see God using someone else. I would venture to say 99.9% of all criticism is insecurity's trying to reinforce its own position.

4. Insecurities may be caused by the rejection or the pain of earlier days. Childhood rejection and rejection of a group or a leader are just a couple. I have already alluded to the life of Jack Hyles, classically illustrating this point. He endured childhood rejection as he watched his drunken father hit his mother, and then as his dad prepared to leave their home, the adolescent boy tried to keep his father by wrapping his arms around his legs and screaming "Daddy, Daddy, please don't leave! Wouldn't you rather have a son than liquor?"

Athey Hyles did not heed the cries of his son; he pushed the boy away, stepped over his body, left the home, and never returned. That feeling of rejection overflowed when the teenage Jack Hyles met his dad and told him he had been called to preach. His drunken father cursed at him, hit him, and embarrassed him in front of hundreds of people on a very busy day in Dallas, Texas. Great insecurity shrouded the life of Dr. Jack Hyles. Pastoring and married at 21 years of age, he faced rejection again from his church people and his convention.

The wonder to me and the great testimony to the Christianity of Dr. Jack Hyles was that he was never a critic. The man who wouldn't criticize anyone was hyper-criticized. His formative years of facing rejection explain why he would not always correct people who seemed out of line.

I remember one time when I went to Brother Hyles and said of someone whose supposed defense of Brother Hyles' ministry was causing great hurt, "So-and-so is creaming your ministry. Why don't you do something?"

"Suppose you have a man with his fingers around your throat choking off your oxygen, and another guy is defending you," he offered by way of explanation. "While the guy who is defending you is ripping those fingers off, he is standing on your toe and hurting your toe! Still, you don't say anything about it because you are so glad he is getting the fingers off your neck. That person about whom you are worried has his foot on my toe, and though it is hurting badly, I can live with a sore toe. But I have to breathe." He was such a man of wisdom, and he possessed an incredible insight and understanding about insecurity—he had faced the terrible pain of insecurity caused by rejection or pain in his life.

5. **It is so very important that parents and teachers and leaders ask for wisdom and love with respect to their followers and their children.** It is hyper-important for parents to be very careful with their words and that they stay married and don't walk out on their children's lives. Some of the most tragic brokenness in our marriages has been caused by children who grew up and could not deal with their rejection. They saw marriage as a secure foundation, and in embracing it, they suffocated the life of their partner. Their partner, for whatever reason, cruelly pushed them away; in so doing, it became just one more rejection in their life. Rejection breeds rejection, breeds rejection, breeds insecurity, breeds insecurity, breeds insecurity.

Parents, love your kids. More importantly, parents, love each other! Kids growing up who weren't loved and secure with parents who loved each other bring incredible difficulties into their marriage, into their families, and into their child rearing. Marriage problems can be repaired, but the greatest difficulty is trying to fix the brokenness of the lives that were the peripheral damages from making bad decisions.

Additionally, teachers need to be careful what they say to their students. Rejection comes in all kinds of sizes and shapes—comparisons, public rebuke, and public putdowns. When having a problem with a child or young person, privately enlist the help of the parents or the principal. If I had my way, it would be against the law ever to publicly humiliate a kid. Humiliating a student might give a teacher control of the classroom for a little while and show he is the person in charge, but that public humiliation will cause problems and insecurities. It is so very important for parents and leaders to beg God for wisdom and love every day with respect to those under their care.

6. All insecurity ultimately comes from leaning on some other person besides the Lord for one's confidence. *"But beware of men: for they will deliver you up to the councils, and they will scourge you in their synagogues."* (Matthew 10:17) The entire tenth chapter of Matthew is a private session of Jesus' teaching His disciples on how to handle the insecurities of leadership. Insecure leaders only grow more insecure the higher they go on the ladder.

As I have already stated, I am a fairly secure, confident person, but truthfully, I have never felt more insecurity than in being the pastor of First Baptist Church of Hammond, Indiana. I know that I am where I am supposed to be. But every single day, I feel like I am residing somewhere between sheer terror and dread! Other than that, life is great!

Some people like to be around a leader because they want to use him to get to leadership. The truth of the matter is that people plug into leadership because it makes them feel better about themselves.

Dr. Rick Finley, the pastor of Fellowship Baptist Church in Durham, North Carolina, said it so succinctly, "I feel the most sorry for some leaders' followers because they get fed nothing but the instability of insecurity." All insecurity ultimately comes from leaning on some other person besides the Lord for confidence.

Matthew 10:1 says, *"And when he had called unto him his twelve disciples, he gave them **power**...."* The word *power* used in this Scripture is the Greek word *exousia*, which means "authority." A pastor is given *exousia* (authority) by both the Lord and by his church members to pastor the church. I have been given authority (power) by both the Lord and by the people of First Baptist Church to pastor this church. God holds me accountable for what is said behind the pulpit of First Baptist Church.

II Timothy 1:7 illustrates a second kind of power. *"For God hath not given us the spirit of fear; but of **power**...."* This word *power* is the same English word *power*, but it is a different Greek word—*dunamis*, from which we derive our modern word "dynamite." *Dunamis* means "energy" or "control." It is the power to accomplish a work within your sphere of influence. God gave to each of His disciples both "authority" *power* and "energy" *power*. God wanted to send them forth with *exousia* (*authority*) and *dunamis* (*control*) for them to possess the strength to exercise control in their arena of influence. God did not give them the spirit of fear; He gave them the spirit of power. Their confidence came from knowing Who gave them their authority to do the work He called them to do.

If God hasn't given a person the spirit of fear, then who has? The answer to that question is not Satan; the correct answer is the person who rejected him. Fear is manifested by asking questions like:

- "Am I going to get the promotion?"
- "Do I have my own parking place?"
- "Is my office close to the boss?"
- "Will I have my own private meeting with the CEO?"

The boss did not call you to the ministry! God did! I personally did not call any of the people who work with me to the ministry. We work together as a team, but God called them to the ministry. Each person who serves with me has his own place of service that God gave to him. If we are going to follow Jesus Christ, then we must understand that Jesus called us to His work—not man!

7. **People who have a difficult time understanding that it is Jesus Who called them must find other people to provide them with protection and security.**

8. **The most confident people are not those who act confidently and powerfully, but those who know and understand their authority boundaries and exercise their energies within those limits.** For example, parents and in-

laws are wonderful people, but they cannot exercise authority in their married children's area of authority. A confident, secure leader exercises *dunamis* (energy power) in an *exousia* (authority power) world. Married children do not have to be angry or ugly with interfering parents. They just need to say kindly, "This is the area of authority God gave to me. These are the children that God gave to us. I appreciate your love and concern, but your love and concern end where our area of authority begins."

Married children have the right to invite their parents into their area of authority. They can ask their parents for advice. They can ask them to baby-sit. Parents can be asked for help in nurturing the grandchildren.

My son-in-law Todd and our daughter Jaclynn now have their own arena of authority as do I. I have said to Todd, "I will never tell you what to do. You may choose to invite me in, and I will consider your request, but I don't ever want to be in conflict with your authority." By the same token, he never steps into my area of authority. That deference builds excellent in-law relationships. That deference is also what makes good human relationships.

9.   **The wasted or abused energy of trying to make others outside of your area of influence submit to you leaves you exhausted, restless, angry, and even ungodly.** Luke 9:49-50 says, *"And John answered and said, Master, we saw one casting out devils in thy name; and we forbad him, because he followeth not with us. And Jesus said unto him, Forbid him not: for he that is not against us is for us."* John was expending so much energy on

deciding who was worthy that he did not have the energy to do the job that he had been given to do! John was too busy telling others whether or not they were qualified to be associated with Jesus! What a waste of time and energy!

10.   Faith is trusting God to bless you inside your area of influence and to protect you from those outside. God will defend the person who stays inside his area of authority. Insecurity tries to find security from those inside his area of influence and in trying to control those outside that area of influence. Only God can give power and influence to an individual. That individual has only the authority that God gives to him. He must let God defend him from everyone outside his sphere of influence and power. Quite simply, as soon as one leaves his area of influence, he leaves God's blessing.

11.   The solution is always found in the simplicity of obedience and followship. Matthew 10 is a wonderful chapter about leadership, and in verses 38 and 39, Jesus says, *"And he that taketh not his cross, and followeth after me, is not worthy of me. He that findeth his life shall lose it: and he that loseth his life for my sake shall find it."* Very simply, follow Jesus wherever He takes you.

When I married at 21 years of age, I was not afraid to be the head of my home. At 23 years of age, I was not afraid to become a father. I never reared my children one day out of fear because they were my kids, and I knew God gave them to me. God held me responsible for rearing our children and empowered me to do what He authorized me to do. *"For it is God which worketh in you both to will and to do of his good pleasure."*

(Philippians 2:13) I will not waste one second leaving my area of influence to try to tell anyone else how to lead. My concern is simply to obey Him and follow Him.

CHAPTER 8

"True leadership cannot be awarded, appointed, or assigned.
It comes only from influence, and that can't be mandated."
— John C. Maxwell

THE CHALLENGES
OF SERVANT LEADERSHIP

"Behold, the third time I am ready to come to you; and I will
not be burdensome to you: for I seek not your's, but you: for the
children ought not to lay up for the parents, but the parents for the
children. And I will very gladly spend and be spent for you; though
the more abundantly I love you, the less I be loved. But be it so, I
did not burden you: nevertheless, being crafty, I caught you with
guile. Did I make a gain of you by any of them whom I sent unto
you? I desired Titus, and with him I sent a brother. Did Titus make

a gain of you? walked we not in the same spirit? walked we not in the same steps? Again, think ye that we excuse ourselves unto you? we speak before God in Christ: but we do all things, dearly beloved, for your edifying. For I fear, lest, when I come, I shall not find you such as I would, and that I shall be found unto you such as ye would not: lest there be debates, envyings, wraths, strifes, backbitings, whisperings, swellings, tumults: And lest, when I come again, my God will humble me among you, and that I shall bewail many which have sinned already, and have not repented of the uncleanness and fornication and lasciviousness which they have committed." (II Corinthians 12:14-21)

Servant leadership is not talking about serving and leading; servant leadership is a Biblical model of leadership with challenges that must be embraced.

1. The challenge of servant leadership is the challenge of stability and self-control. The test of leadership is to lead under adverse circumstances. Leadership is not really tested when everything is going well. The test of a leader is how he handles himself in particular, as well as the followers, when adverse circumstances bare down upon them.

"Leaders must endure not only their own tragedies but those of others as well. Empathy and wisdom on such occasions become human building blocks, creating loyalty and trust."[1]

The infamous story of Ziklag is found in I Samuel 30. David has fled from the machinations of Saul, has finally found a place of refuge in the city of Ziklag, and Saul has ended his pursuit. *"And it came to pass, when David and his men were come to Ziklag on the third day, that the Amalekites had invaded the south, and Ziklag, and smitten Ziklag, and burned it with fire; And had taken the women captives, that were therein: they slew not any, either great or small, but carried them away, and went on their way. So David and his men came to the city, and, behold, it was burned with fire; and their wives, and their sons, and their daughters, were taken captives. Then David and the people that were with him lifted up their voice and wept, until they had no more power to weep. And David's two wives were taken captives, Ahinoam the Jezreelitess, and Abigail the wife of Nabal the Carmelite."* (I Samuel 30:1-5) Everyone had suffered some type of loss, and most assuredly, David was suffering as much as anyone else was suffering. His family had been taken captive, and his children were also gone.

Verse 6 reveals a critical key to the servant leader. *"And David was greatly distressed; for the people spake of stoning him, because the soul of all the people was grieved, every man for his sons and for his daughters:* **but David encouraged himself in the LORD his God."** With servant leadership, the issue of who comes first when things have to be cared for must be carefully evaluated. Always the issue of "How do I prioritize my pain when I am hurting as much as the people I am trying to lead?" must be addressed. David, as the servant leader, had a very difficult human decision to make.

Servant leaders are not necessarily better quality physical specimens. They suffer from the same kinds of aches and pains; they do not necessarily possess a high pain tolerance or threshold. They do not enjoy watching the pain and anguish of their loved ones. Servant leaders possess the same emotions as everyone else does.

The Bible says of Jesus Christ that He was in all points tempted like as we are, and the Bible says He was touched with the feeling of our infirmities. Not only did He face a spiritual war with Satan, but His feelings vibrated to the same

> "The leadership about which Jesus speaks is of a radically different kind from the leadership offered by the world. It is a servant leadership—in which the leader is a vulnerable servant who needs the people as much as they need him.[2]

intensity level that man's feelings vibrate. His anguish would have been a feeling that could have led to vengeance; after all, anguish is a precursor to vengeance. One doesn't necessarily first feel vengeance; he first feels incredible injury before he becomes bitter and wants to wreak vengeance. I have no doubt that Jesus felt terrible injury as well as terrible pain.

King David felt just as much bereavement as his people did. However, the people were not sympathetic; they became vengeful and desired to punish David because he supposedly "allowed" the incursion of the Amalekites. At times like this, the servant leader must exercise incredible self-control. To exercise that control, "...*David encouraged himself in the* LORD *his God.*" David knew that it is very difficult to lead others when one cannot lead himself. At this point of angst in his life, King David realized he had nobody to follow except himself. David decided to lead the only person who would follow—him.

As he began leading himself, the focus of the account very quickly changes.

"*...but David encouraged himself in the LORD his God. And David said to Abiathar the priest, Ahimelech's son, I pray thee, bring me hither the ephod. And Abiathar brought thither the ephod to David. And David enquired at the LORD, saying, Shall I pursue after this troop? shall I overtake them? And he answered him, Pursue: for thou shalt surely overtake them, and without fail recover all. So David went, he and the six hundred men that were with him....*" (I Samuel 30:6-9) When the leader leads himself, his followers will fall into line again. They just need a leader who can rally himself in the critical times. David possessed servant leadership capabilities.

"When storms strike individuals, a leader who responds with genuine concern and calm establishes his leadership."[3]

- Servant leadership possesses the ability to lead the one who is probably the most distressed.
- Servant leadership is the ability of the leader to maintain his equilibrium when everyone else has lost his.
- Servant leadership is the leader's ability to walk a straight line, without veering left and right, and maintaining his directional momentum. "The leader with a crystallized calling can lead with resolve, urgency, and persistence."[4]

Some people are promoted to positions of leadership because of charisma or abilities. However, when they are promoted to a position in management, they stumble terribly because they had been in a secure environment with no real pressures.

Many people can handle the rhythm of an assembly line very well and do an excellent job with adjusting the nuts and bolts of the machinery. When they have to take the corporate pressure that goes hand-in-hand with leadership, they buckle terribly because they never learned to develop the internal mechanism that says, "I can lead one person without fail, and that one person is me."

Whether leading takes place in a home or in a marriage or in a church or in the workplace, the bottom line is the leader must learn to lead himself. That person will listen to his inner voice, be able to distract himself from his internal pain, and recognize what needs to be done.

You are as good of a leader as you can maintain your stability during very unstable times. If God wants to prove that you are a great leader, He will more than likely place you in a position of extreme instability where everyone can watch how stable you are.

I think about the unlikelihood of Dr. Jack Hyles coming to First Baptist Church of Hammond. This American Baptist Church was not exactly familiar with his Southern Texas boy style of preaching. As a result, he was confronted with a big showdown a year later. Sometimes great leaders face conflicts like that to demonstrate their great leadership abilities. If you do not like adverse conditions, don't ever accept a leadership position. Strong leaders see adversity as a time to shine. Servant leadership possesses the ability to bring stability to those times of conflict and instability.

2.   **The challenge of servant leadership is the challenge**

of maintaining meekness and gentleness. According to Exodus 4:14-16, Aaron had been given to Moses as his spokesperson. *"And the anger of the LORD was kindled against Moses, and he said, Is not Aaron the Levite thy brother? I know that he can speak well. And also, behold, he cometh forth to meet thee: and when he seeth thee, he will be glad in his heart. And thou shalt speak unto him, and put words in his mouth: and I will be with thy mouth, and with his mouth, and will teach you what ye shall do. And he shall be thy spokesman unto the people: and he shall be, even he shall be to thee instead of a mouth, and thou shalt be to him instead of God."*

In Numbers 12:1-15, Miriam and Aaron (Moses' sister and brother) rebuked their leader, and in doing so, both stepped out of their God-given positions of leadership. In a sense Aaron was saying that he knew more than God did.

"And Miriam and Aaron spake against Moses because of the Ethiopian woman whom he had married: for he had married an Ethiopian woman. And they said, Hath the LORD indeed spoken only by Moses? hath he not spoken also by us? And the LORD heard it. **(Now the man Moses was very meek, above all the men which were upon the face of the earth.)** *And the LORD spake suddenly unto Moses, and unto Aaron, and unto Miriam, Come out ye three unto the tabernacle of the congregation. And they three came out. And the LORD came down in the pillar of the cloud, and stood in the door of the tabernacle, and called Aaron and Miriam: and they both came forth. And he said, Hear now my words: If there be a prophet among you, I the LORD will make myself known unto him in a vision, and will speak unto him in a dream. My ser-*

vant Moses is not so, who is faithful in all mine house. With him will I speak mouth to mouth, even apparently, and not in dark speeches; and the similitude of the LORD shall he behold: wherefore then were ye not afraid to speak against my servant Moses? And the anger of the LORD was kindled against them; and he departed. And the cloud departed from off the tabernacle; and, behold, Miriam became leprous, white as snow: and Aaron looked upon Miriam, and, behold, she was leprous. And Aaron said unto Moses, Alas, my lord, I beseech thee, lay not the sin upon us, wherein we have done foolishly, and wherein we have sinned. Let her not be as one dead, of whom the flesh is half consumed when he cometh out of his mother's womb. And Moses cried unto the Lord, saying, Heal her now, O God, I beseech thee. And the LORD said unto Moses, If her father had but spit in her face, should she not be ashamed seven days? let her be shut out from the camp seven days, and after that let her be received in again. And Miriam was shut out from the camp seven days: and the people journeyed not till Miriam was brought in again."

In this very powerful story, Moses was being rebuked by his brother and sister, being accused of taking too much upon himself, and being reprimanded for thinking he knew exactly what God wanted the children of Israel to do. The truth is, Moses hadn't done anything; He had told Aaron what to say. Now Aaron wanted to bypass Moses and just go directly to God himself. Miriam joined Aaron in the censuring of their brother. Their sudden revolt against Moses stemmed from a jealousy issue—they did not like whom he chose to marry. True, Moses went outside of the Jewish arena to marry an

Ethiopian woman. By all the legal laws, the brother-and-sister team felt they had a right to rebuke their leader.

However, not one time in any way in this passage of Scripture did Moses defend himself. Moses didn't say one word, speak one word of rebuke or correction, respond, or analyze the situation. He let God deal with his sister, and when she was smitten with leprosy, Aaron begged Moses for help. Aaron knew that Moses was the only man to whom God would listen. Amazing how desperate circumstances brought Aaron and Miriam to the only one who could help.

Had I been the leader in this situation, I probably would have snapped, "I thought you could get answers directly from God yourself. You are on your own! Best of luck to you!" But the meekness of Moses demonstrates profoundly his servant leadership. Servant leader, can you remain gentle in tumultuous times? The word *meekness* is the Hebrew word meaning "gentle." Can you remain gentle like Moses when your close associates become indignant or critical and challenge your position of authority? Do you have enough meekness to say, "Tell me what is on your heart."

If you accept a position of leadership and follow a Scriptural model, it is vital to develop the gentleness mandated by Scripture in that place of leadership. Far too many people want to attain a place of leadership first and then see if they can later add the qualities that make a good leader. In the meanwhile, all of the followers suffer.

That lack is precisely why some pastors serve in several works before they finally settle in to one. They initially accepted a position of leadership without first learning the challenge of gentleness or of self-control. They lost control too many times, and there were far too many tug-of-wars with angry words and harshness. What immaturity!

Servant leadership works to develop the areas that nobody else seemingly wants to develop. A preacher boy never says, "God, give me gentleness." Rather, he prays, "Give me a vision of reaching the world!" God knows that young man doesn't have the self-control to handle the people when they question his leadership ability.

In your future dreams, you don't picture the people you love opposing you. In your dreams, you don't picture people in your family opposing you. In your dreams, you don't picture the people with whom you work opposing you or challenging your leadership. Those times will inevitably come. Thankfully, servant leadership has a tremendous role model to follow in Moses, who *"was very meek, above all the men which were upon the face of the earth."*

3.   **The challenge of servant leadership is the challenge of principled obedience and integrity.** To follow your integrity and be obedient to a principle rather than to follow your emotion and what seems to be the natural way to react is a challenge.

Lot's separation from Abraham is often overlooked because it is a part of another great story. *"And there was a strife between the herdmen of Abram's cattle and the herdmen of Lot's cattle: and the Canaanite and the Perizzite dwelled then in the land. And Abram said unto Lot, Let there be no strife, I pray thee, between me and thee, and between my herdmen and thy herdmen; for we be brethren."* (Genesis 13:7, 8) Most definitely Lot should not have allowed this strife to develop.

Genesis 14:1 continues, *"And it came to pass in the days of Amraphel king of Shinar, Arioch king of Ellasar, Chedorlaomer king of Elam, and Tidal king of nations; That these made war with Bera king of Sodom, and with Birsha king of Gomorrah, Shinab king of Admah, and Shemeber king of Zeboiim, and the king of Bela, which is Zoar. All these were joined together in the vale of Siddim, which is the salt sea. Twelve years they served Chedorlaomer, and in the thirteenth year they rebelled....And they took all the goods of Sodom and Gomorrah, and all their victuals, and went their way. And they took Lot, Abram's brother's son, who dwelt in Sodom, and his goods, and departed."* (Genesis 14:1-4, 11, 12) Lot and his family were caught in the middle of a Canaanite war. Lot hated the life he was living in the Sodomite cities of Sodom and Gomorrah. II Peter 2:7-8 says, *"And delivered just Lot, vexed with the filthy conversation of the wicked. (For that righteous man dwelling among them, in seeing and hearing, vexed his righteous soul from day to day with their unlawful deeds)."* Lot would ultimately lose everything dear to him including his wife because he chose to move away from Abraham. He paid a terrible price because he could not lead his followers.

When Abraham heard about the capture of his nephew, he illustrated great leadership. Genesis 14:14 continues, *"And when Abram heard that his brother was taken captive, he armed his trained servants, born in his own house, three hundred and eighteen, and pursued them unto Dan. And he divided himself against them, he and his servants, by night, and smote them, and pursued them unto Hobah, which is on the left hand of Damascus. And he brought back all the goods, and also brought again his brother Lot, and his goods, and the women also, and the people."* Abraham did not rejoice over Lot's misfortune and say, "It serves him right. Any relative of mine who wants to live in Sodom should be taken captive! That is justice." No! Not Abraham! He displayed servant leadership; he rallied his men in defense of his nephew. He was a servant leader who was principled in his integrity. He did not allow family feuds and petty arguments to decide his level of integrity. A man's personal integrity demands professional leadership.

Many children suffer in their homes because they have a parent or even two parents where servant leadership is not present. There is only antagonistic leadership. Holding grudges is commonplace. A servant leader sets aside petty squabbles that divide family and friends to fight for a just cause.

The test of servant leadership is to set aside one's own hurt and lead others in a just cause. I Peter 2:21–3:1, 7 should stir the Christian's heart to action. *"For even hereunto were ye called: because Christ also suffered for us, leaving us an example, that ye should follow his steps:* [the steps of suffering] *Who did no sin, neither was guile* [deceptiveness or hypocrisy] *found in his mouth: Who, when he was reviled* [called names], *reviled not again; when he suffered* [put up with the way people threatened him], *he threatened not; but committed himself to him that judgeth righteously: Who his own self bare our sins in his own body on the tree, that we, being dead to sins, should live unto righteousness: by whose stripes ye were healed. For ye were as sheep going astray; but are now returned unto the Shepherd and Bishop of your souls. Likewise* [Jesus did not revile, did not threaten, and did not act hypocritically], *ye wives, be in subjection to your own husbands; that, if any obey not the word* [if they threaten, revile or try to harm you and don't obey the word], *they also may without the word be won by the conversation* [lifestyle] *of the wives;... Likewise, ye husbands, dwell with them according to knowledge, giving honour unto the wife, as unto the weaker vessel, and as being heirs together of the grace of life; that your prayers be not hindered."* What exactly are these verses teaching?

Can you set aside your own hurt for the good of the cause? Husband and wife, can you set aside your own hurts to give your children a platform of stability called a secure home while you privately figure out how you are going to handle the disputes within your marriage? Many people who have disputes in their marriage rear fabulous kids. Why? Because their kids are never victimized by their parents driving wedges between them and forcing them to choose one parent over another. There is a greater cause than who wins the arguments! Parents, put aside your petty differences and rear your kids! It's time to show some servant leadership.

Perhaps the disputes will never be ironed out, but for the greater cause of the children, it's time for some parents to lay down their weapons. The servant leader always looks at the the greater cause of the people involved. Sadly, sometimes we miss those greater causes, and that is truly the challenge of servant leadership. No matter how badly you hurt, no matter how badly frustrated you are, and no matter how much angst you have about the rights and wrongs being violated in your own personal world, the servant leader focuses on the greater cause. For Abraham, the greater cause was Lot and his family. Abraham illustrated servant leadership which is limited only by one's ability to swallow his pride and look to the greater cause.

4. **The challenge of servant leadership is the challenge of inverse love and sacrifice.** In II Corinthians 12:15 the Bible states, *"And I will **very gladly spend** and be spent for you; though the more abundantly I love you, the less I be loved."* A person sacrificially gives expressions of love. The challenge that comes is that the receiver seldom, if ever, returns a compensatory amount or equal measure to the giver. This concept is more difficult to understand.

Allow me to illustrate by means of a quotation by Dr. Bob Jones, Sr. Upon hearing the news that someone was criticizing his ministry, Dr. Bob said, "I don't know why he hates me so much; I never did anything for him."

I first heard that statement used in a meeting with Brother Hyles. He had sacrificially given tens of thousands of dollars to a pastor who was now viciously attacking him. I asked, "Didn't you just give him thousands of dollars? Why is he doing that?"

My father-in-law said, "Let me share something I heard from Dr. Bob Jones, Sr.: 'I don't know why so-and-so hates me so much; I never did anything for him.'" As I chuckled, he said, "Let me teach you a great principle of leadership for someday when you need it. The more you do for people, the more likely you will be the recipient of their displeasure someday."

That conversation took place years before I became a bus captain. I had helped several families on that bus route with financial needs, and I had also noticed that the more I helped the people, the less the children rode the bus to church. One particular day a woman I had never before seen found me and asked for financial help. She said, "I have never asked you before, but I need your help. We need $340 to pay our gas and electric bill."

I took a deep breath and said, "Ma'am, I'm sorry, but I am not going to pay your bill. I have paid bills for several people, and now their children no longer ride my bus. I like your kids, and I want to keep them on my bus. I'm sorry, but I cannot pay your bills." Those children never stopped riding my bus!

Don't get me wrong; I believe in being very generous. I have paid hundreds of thousands of dollars worth of people's bills in the years I have been in this ministry. If I hear someone has a need, I try to do everything in my power I can to help that person.

I hadn't been a pastor more than a month when a dear pastor friend of mine called and asked for help. "Absolutely I will help you," I replied. "You are my dear friend, and I believe you would help me if I were in trouble. I am going to help you." Less than six months later, that man leveled a vicious attack at me and First Baptist Church. I just shook my head in disbelief. The only person on staff who knew I had done any-thing about that man's need asked, "What is so-and-so's prob-lem?"

"I gave him some money," I said truthfully.

"That sure figures," he agreed. "You know what Brother Hyles used to say...."

I still believe we should be generous and helpful, and I am not worried about a disgruntled person. However, I am using that story to illustrate that when you start giving and helping, an inverse proportion of love will generally not be returned. A compensatory measure will not be expected to be returned because servant leadership realizes that today is not the time to receive rewards. Heaven is rewarding time.

The person who cannot relate to that principle will never make a very good servant leader. The Bible says in Proverbs 19:17, *"He that hath pity upon the poor lendeth unto the* LORD...." When you fill a need, you are making a loan to God, and God promises in the book of Mark that He will return interest on that loan. I suggest that, as a servant leader, you make invest-ments in God's bank and give without hoping to receive returns on this earth. A servant leader must understand that he is on earth to serve, and his real compensation is a heaven-ly reward.

5.   The challenge of servant leadership is the challenge of discovering the proper language of love and leadership. A servant leader must understand that a proper language must be communicated. The author Gary Chapman wrote a series of books on marriage, and one book addressed the language of

love. One statement he wrote is, "Happiness in a relationship is the by-product of feeling loved." I often say as I counsel couples, "You must learn what your spouse grasps about love."

The typical comment I hear from many men is, "I work hard; I put money in the checkbook; I put food on the table; I keep the bills paid; we drive a nice car; we have nice clothes in the closet; the kids are well-maintained; and I don't understand why our marriage stinks." The man who says this has done all of the loving that a man is required to do. I say to that man's wife, "He may not be speaking the love language you understand, but you need to try to understand his language!" A wise wife seeks to understand her husband's expressions of love. The wise husband will seek to understand his wife's language of love if he really wants to take his marriage to the next level of greatness. He can't just simply say, "This is how I love; take this $50 bill and be happy."

So many men erroneously think that some money will solve a multitude of problems. To be sure, make the denominations big enough, and it can take care of quite a few problems! However, nothing compares to understanding the love language of the person you love.

Understanding the language of love is no different than understanding any other language. However, it can be a foreign language or concept to many people. Learning a language that you have never before learned properly can be difficult.

Languages have barriers that must be crossed. Crossing these barriers is not a matter of sincerity or a matter of desire. It is not based on the presence or the absence of love. It is the matter of whether or not you can discern or acquire the language that is best understood. Great followers seek, find, and receive the language of the leader. A great leader will search until he discovers the language that communicates his love.

For example, teenagers have a love language that they understand which is altogether different from the love language of little children. The language of love is altogether different for different people. Allow me to illustrate. A four-year-old boy sitting on his mother's lap says, "Mommy, when I grow up, I want to marry you!" What a wonderful feeling! However, when he is 14, don't remind him of that promise because that is no longer the language of love he understands! I remember Dr. Hyles saying, "The worst sight a 14 year old can see is two 40-year-old lips coming at him!" The language of love varies as one matures.

Just as there is a language of love for husbands and wives, a language of love for teenagers, a language of love for children, etc., the servant leader must understand the language of loving God and serving Him. Servant leadership implies that the servant leader is both serving people as he leads, but also serving God foremost. This language of God is very important, and many people do not understand this love language of God. God has written 66 Books for us and has given us a hard copy so we can discern His love language. God does not get moved deeply by what *we* think He would like. Most assuredly, God is moved by some things, and I want to share some of His languages of love toward man.

THE LANGUAGE OF TIMING

In Exodus 2 the Bible says that Moses felt that the children of Israel would easily comprehend that he was going to be their deliverer. *"And it came to pass in those days, when Moses was grown, that he went out unto his brethren, and looked on their burdens: and he spied an Egyptian smiting an Hebrew, one of his brethren. And he looked this way and that way, and when he saw that there was no man, he slew the Egyptian, and hid him in the sand. And when he went out the second day, behold, two men of the Hebrews strove together: and he said to him that did the wrong, Wherefore smitest thou thy fellow? And he said, Who made thee a prince and a judge over us?…"* (Exodus 2:11-14) Moses did not really consult with God about His timing, and when he felt the need for a deliverer arose, Moses volunteered, took matters into his own hands, and killed a man.

In the book of Exodus, Moses had to record God's judgments, and one of them stated the payment required for killing a man and then hiding the body was the death penalty. It must have been very difficult for Moses to write those words, knowing that he had hidden a murder once.

Ecclesiastes 3:1 says, *"To every thing there is a season, and a* **time** *to every purpose under the heaven."* Verse 11 continues, *"He hath made every thing beautiful in his time.…"* One language that God surely understands is the language of people who can be patient in their waiting on His timing.

One of the tremendous insults we give to God is not insincerity, but that we either get ahead of God or we won't stay up with God. God can move at a rapid pace, but God never moves at a pace that is beyond the capability of maintaining a rhythm and a cadence with all His other duties. God was saying to Moses, "It is not time for you yet. You are not yet ready because you are not willing to take orders."

Many sins involve timing problems. For instance, nothing is wrong with a couple's desire to marry. However, perhaps the parents want the couple to wait for a period of time. The duo does not want to wait, but if they are to have their parents' blessing, they will wait. The issue isn't whether or not they should get married; the issue is a timing issue. More than likely, this young couple should get married, but they need to trust that, in God's timing, He will make everything beautiful.

So if God has made everything beautiful in His time, what happens when you get out of the timing of God? The situation turns ugly.

A beautiful young lady who epitomizes this very issue sat in my office. I pleaded with her to wait to get married. "I am not trying to run your life," I appealed earnestly. "My request is not a control issue at all; trust me, it is a timing issue. Would you just give it a little longer? You are not yet ready to get married."

"With all due respect, Pastor Schaap," she retorted, "I am madly in love with the man of my dreams, and I am going to get married with or without your blessing."

Eighteen months later she came to see me and said, "Tell me this: why didn't I listen to you? Not listening to you was the stupidest thing I ever did." The marriage had turned ugly.

Immature people are not ready to carry the load that will be placed on them in marriage. No amount of verbiage from the mouth of a caring pastor or loving parents will sink in and make a couple understand that counseling them to wait is not about controlling their lives. We are not trying to dictate who or who not to marry. Neither are we trying to dictate how or how not to run their lives. We may be clumsy at stating that issues involve timing—not a matter of whether or not you will get married.

So many fine marriages should not end in divorce, and the couple would not have sought a divorce if they would have just understood that the language God appreciates is the language of "do it on My schedule—not yours."

Allow me to share another timing issue. A young couple in their middle twenties, who has delayed marriage, love each other, are officially engaged, and plan to get married, so what is wrong with their being intimate? Trust a pastor who counsels these kinds of situations more often than you can imagine. That timing issue will come back to haunt that couple; it will have a greater backlash than their present love can withstand.

The Biblical illustration for this principle about ignoring the timing of God is Tamar and Amnon, who was deceived by his friend, Jonadab. Amnon, the eldest son of King David and Ahinoam, loved his half-sister Tamar, who was the daughter of King David and Maacah. In Bible times, it would have been legal and acceptable for them to marry, but that is not the lesson to be learned. The issue is that Amnon chose to ignore a procedure he could have followed to do right by Tamar.

Instead he listened to the counsel of Jonadab and raped his half-sister instead of honorably requesting for her to be his wife. Immediately after forcing her, the emotion of love turned 180 degrees to hate and increased exponentially in intensity. The Bible says, *"Then Amnon hated her **exceedingly**; so that the hatred wherewith he hated her was greater than the love wherewith he had loved her...."* (II Samuel 13:15)

To some, this incident is just another Bible story. However, God did not include this story in the Bible to shame David or Tamar or even Amnon. A Biblical principle was violated when the timing of God was ignored. A couple is so in love. He says, "We are getting married. Why wait? If you love me...." Some years later into the marriage, one of the couple will likely say, "I hate my spouse. I never did love my spouse. I didn't love my spouse back then either."

The timing was wrong, and a language that God loves very much is the language of timing. A person must yield to God and say, "I will do anything You want—**whenever** You want me to."

The flip side of the language of timing is when people continuously postpone serving God. Moses wasted nearly two-thirds of his life before he was finally willing to listen to God. Please don't do the same and wait until two-thirds of your life is done before you listen to the call of God. Samuel gave his heart to God as a little boy. When God called, Samuel said, *"...Speak; for thy servant heareth."* (I Samuel 3:10)

In reference to the language of timing, may I also suggest to young couples who get married to take a goodly amount of time to get their marriage on sure footing before having children. Be patient, and let the children come into an established home. I cannot stress how important it is to be careful and wise in regard to timing in the matter of falling in love and in the matter of welcoming children into your home.

THE LANGUAGE OF FAITH

Forty years have passed in Moses' life, and God is calling him to do His work in Exodus chapter 4. *"And Moses said unto the LORD, O my Lord, I am not eloquent, neither heretofore, nor since thou hast spoken unto thy servant: but I am slow of speech, and of a slow tongue. And the LORD said unto him, Who hath made man's mouth? or who maketh the dumb, or deaf, or the seeing, or the blind? have not I the LORD? Now therefore go, and I will be with thy mouth, and teach thee what thou shalt say. And he said, O my Lord, send, I pray thee, by the hand of him whom thou wilt send. And the anger of the LORD was kindled against Moses...."* (Exodus 4:10-14)

Obviously God does not like the language of Moses in this passage! This Scripture illustrates exactly what faith isn't. Faith is not hiding behind one's perceived human weaknesses as an excuse not to obey God. Self-deprecation is being used as an excuse not to do what God told Moses to do. Every time you use yourself as a reason for why you won't do what God says, it is always a language that angers God.

Faith always says, "Yes, God!" God hates it when a man hides behind his supposed weaknesses. Every time man tells

God why he "won't" because of something he thinks he "can't," "can't" to God means "won't." God says, "The problem is all about **you**, isn't it?" The truth is that it is all about God! If He tells us to go or to do, He will make up the deficit. God is always the measure of what we need.

If a person only has one percent to offer God, God is the other needed ninety-nine percent! I learned this wonderful principle as a college student listening to preachers preach on this subject. I realized my job was to convince God that I needed Him completely and to tell Him that I was willing to do anything—as long as He went with me! God gives to every person strengths, gifts, abilities, and talents. Don't sell yourself short to God because He is a 100-percent God!

THE LANGUAGE OF INTERCESSION

"And the LORD said unto Moses, I have seen this people, and, behold, it is a stiffnecked people: Now therefore let me alone, that my wrath may wax hot against them, and that I may consume them: and I will make of thee a great nation. And Moses besought the LORD his God, and said, LORD, why doth thy wrath wax hot against thy people, which thou hast brought forth out of the land of Egypt with great power, and with a mighty hand? Wherefore should the Egyptians speak, and say, For mischief did he bring them out, to slay them in the mountains, and to consume them from the face of the earth? Turn from thy fierce wrath, and repent of this evil against thy people. Remember Abraham, Isaac, and Israel, thy servants, to whom thou swarest by thine own self, and saidst unto

them, I will multiply your seed as the stars of heaven, and all this land that I have spoken of will I give unto your seed, and they shall inherit it for ever. And the LORD *repented of the evil which he thought to do unto his people."* (Exodus 32:9-14)

In this amazing conversation between God and a man, the mortal man Moses told Almighty God to repent and get right with Himself! Was God displeased with the reprimand of Moses? Does this passage say that the anger of the Lord was kindled against Moses? No! God was not at all perturbed or disappointed with Moses because Moses was speaking a language that God understands, loves, and wants to hear from His children.

That same love language is illustrated again in verses 31 through 33 which say, *"And Moses returned unto the* LORD, *and said, Oh, this people have sinned a great sin, and have made them gods of gold. Yet now, if thou wilt forgive their sin—; and if not, blot me, I pray thee, out of thy book which thou hast written. And the* LORD *said unto Moses, Whosoever hath sinned against me, him will I blot out of my book."*

This beautiful language that God loves to hear is the language of intercession—or the language of substitutionary blame. God loves it when someone says, "Lord, I think You have a right to be angry, but I would like You to blame me instead." The reason why that language is so pleasing to God is that it is the language of Jesus Christ, the Author of salvation. The Son of God took the blame for the sins of mankind because God did not want to send them to Hell. Jesus suffered Hell for all mankind.

When someone takes substitutionary blame and intercedes, that word *intercede* means "to make a deal with God on behalf of someone who doesn't deserve it." When God hears a human being taking blame that is not his to take in an attempt to stave off His anger, He loves it! That intercession reminds Him of His own Son of God communicating with Him. The language of intercession is rare.

THE LANGUAGE OF INTIMATE DESIRE

"And Moses said unto the LORD, See, thou sayest unto me, Bring up this people: and thou hast not let me know whom thou wilt send with me. Yet thou hast said, I know thee by name, and thou hast also found grace in my sight. Now therefore, I pray thee, if I have found grace in thy sight, shew me now thy way, that I may know thee, that I may find grace in thy sight: and consider that this nation is thy people. And he said, My presence shall go with thee, and I will give thee rest. And he said unto him, If thy presence go not with me, carry us not up hence. For wherein shall it be known here that I and thy people have found grace in thy sight? is it not in that thou goest with us? so shall we be separated, I and thy people, from all the people that are upon the face of the earth. And the LORD said unto Moses, I will do this thing also that thou hast spoken: for thou hast found grace in my sight, and I know thee by name. And he said, I beseech thee, shew me thy glory. And he said, I will make all my goodness pass before thee, and I will proclaim the name of the LORD before thee; and will be gracious to whom I will be gracious, and will shew mercy on whom I will shew mercy. And he said, Thou canst

not see my face: for there shall no man see me, and live. And the LORD said, Behold, there is a place by me, and thou shalt stand upon a rock: And it shall come to pass, while my glory passeth by, that I will put thee in a clift of the rock, and will cover thee with my hand while I pass by: And I will take away mine hand, and thou shalt see my back parts: but my face shall not be seen." (Exodus 33:12-23)

Moses had become very weary in the journey, and he asked God for a favor. "Would You let me see You, God?" God responds to the language of intimate desire, and God answered Moses' heartfelt request. God placed Moses safely in a cleft in the rock, and as He walked past, He placed His hand over that fissure. As soon as God walked past, He took away His hand and allowed Moses a glimpse of His presence. So many miss the simplicity of this language of intimate desire. It is the language of a man telling God his innermost desires— "God, what I really want is You."

I have no doubt when Fanny Crosby penned the words to the wonderful hymn "Draw Me Nearer," her heart's desire was to know God intimately and personally. The love language of God is incredibly, phenomenally, wonderfully real, and His heart's desire is to know each one of us intimately and personally.

Oh, the pure delight of a single hour
That before Thy throne I spend,
When I kneel in prayer, and with Thee, my God,
I commune as friend with friend!
Draw me nearer, nearer, blessed Lord,

To the cross where Thou hast died;
Draw me nearer, nearer, nearer, blessed Lord,
To Thy precious, bleeding side.

CHAPTER 9

> *"The leader must know, must know he knows,*
> *and must be able to make it abundantly clear*
> *to those about him that he knows."*
> *– Clarence B. Randall*

THE LANGUAGE OF
LEADERSHIP TO FOLLOWSHIP

The challenge of leaders is in discovering the proper language of love and leadership. To a leader who is a servant, the struggle is how does one communicate in a language his followers understand? The language of leadership and the language of serving embrace a two-way direction. It looks one-way toward God. As a servant leader I represent God; therefore, I have to understand His language.

A leader cannot help his followers until he is first on the right wavelength with God. Moses is as an example of a man who was on the correct wavelength with God. He understood the languages that God most understands. The leader who understands those languages and participates in that language with God will find himself in a tremendous zone of blessing with God. Allow me to share those languages of servant leadership from the life of Jesus Christ. The language of the leader to the follower can be understood through three powerful illustrations from the life of Christ.

THE LANGUAGE OF COMPASSION

"And it came to pass, that, when Jesus was returned, the people gladly received him: for they were all waiting for him. And, behold, there came a man named Jairus, and he was a ruler of the synagogue: and he fell down at Jesus' feet, and besought him that he would come into his house: For he had one only daughter, about twelve years of age, and she lay a dying. But as he went the people thronged him. And a woman having an issue of blood twelve years, which had spent all her living upon physicians, neither could be healed of any, Came behind him, and touched the border of his garment: and immediately her issue of blood stanched. And Jesus said, Who touched me? When all denied, Peter and they that were with him said, Master, the multitude throng thee and press thee, and sayest thou, Who touched me? And Jesus said, Somebody hath touched me: for I perceive that virtue [the word virtue means "energy" or "strength"] is gone out of me. And when the woman

saw that she was not hid, she came trembling, and falling down before him, she declared unto him before all the people for what cause she had touched him, and how she was healed immediately." (Luke 8:40-47)

While on His way to help one man's only daughter, a daughter of Israel comes to Him also seeking help. Though He is on his way to heal someone else, He demonstrates compassion and pauses to help this lady. This account shows a very vivid illustration of a language understood by all as the language of compassion.

Compassion is first "the ability to be moved by the hurts and heartaches of others," and secondly, "it is the ability to **act** when confronted with the hurts and heartaches of others." Many people possess the first part of that definition; they are moved by the hurts and heartaches of others. But what distinguishes compassion from just simple sympathy or empathy is the ability to act on the hurts of others.

To be sure, as the pastor of this church, I want the people of First Baptist Church of Hammond, Indiana, to feel the hurts of others. But, I also want them to do something about those hurts. That action distinguishes the language of love and compassion, whether you do something financially, with your time, with your spoken words, or via written expressions. "Servant leaders are healers in the sense of making whole by helping others to a larger and nobler vision and purpose than they would be likely to attain for themselves."[1]

THE LANGUAGE OF PARTNERSHIP

"And the seventy returned again with joy, saying, Lord, even the devils are subject unto us through thy name. And he said unto them, I beheld Satan as lightning fall from heaven. Behold, I give unto you power to tread on serpents and scorpions, and over all the power of the enemy: and nothing shall by any means hurt you." (Luke 10:17-19)

Jesus Christ teaches that what followers would like to hear expressed is simply, "Do you care about me, and can we work together as a team?" People do not want to be spectators! Many churches make a mistake by addressing spectators in their services rather than nurturing participants.

Nurturing has the ability to transform people's lives. Nurturing benefits everyone. Who wouldn't be more secure and motivated when his leader *believes* in him, *encourages* him, *shares* with him, and *trusts* him?[2]

Partnership is very important, whether it is a father to a family or whether it is a pastor to a church, because partnership is all about getting involved. Getting followers involved as soon as possible in the work of God is vital and allows people the opportunity of working together as a team.

THE LANGUAGE OF EMPOWERMENT

"And Jesus came and spake unto them, saying, All power is given unto me in heaven and in earth. Go ye therefore, and teach all nations...." (Matthew 28:18, 19)

"And *I thank Christ Jesus **our** Lord, who hath enabled **me**, for that he counted **me** faithful, putting **me** into the ministry."* I Timothy 1:12 is an intensely personal verse that is saying "God believes in me! Jesus Christ believes in me!" What followers want to know is: "Do you believe in me enough to actually put your weight on me?" It is one thing to say, "I love you, and I am for you." It is yet another thing to say, "Here are the keys to the church bus, and here are the resources you will need. Go for it! Build a bus route to the glory of God!"

Such trust arouses reactions like

- "Do you really believe in me enough to actually put your weight on me?
- Do you trust me with a bus route?
- Do you trust me with a Sunday school class of boys or girls?"

By empowering people, great works can be done.

A pastor's staff wants and needs to be empowered by the pastor. A church needs to be empowered by those who oversee certain areas of responsibility. Acts 1:8 says, *"But ye shall receive power, after that the Holy Ghost is come upon you...."* When the Holy Ghost came upon the leaders in Acts, they did receive that power. With empowerment comes His enabling. Nothing is quite as powerful as the servant leader who says to his people, "I am sensitive and able to respond to the hurts and heartaches of your life. I will act on them. Secondly, I want to partner with you. I would like to go into the business of serving God with you. I would like us to work together as a team. Thirdly, I can empower you by giving you responsibility, authority, and resources." That empowerment is what Jesus Christ teaches us is the language of love from a servant leader to his followers.

One of the most delicate issues of servant leadership involves the transfer of followers to new or different leaders. The negative of growth is dividing an area of leadership which, of course, involves people and giving those people, who have felt your compassion, partnership, and empowerment, to another leader. It then becomes his responsibility to nurture and care for those people. In the case of First Baptist Church of Hammond, I expect those people to continue to be the recipients of the language of servant leadership as though I were still their servant leader.

That issue was my concern when Dr. Jack Hyles died. First Baptist Church of Hammond was such a strong, happy church because so many people felt incredibly loved by their servant-pastor, Brother Hyles. I often listened to him fret over turning the ministry over to a younger man. He felt that a younger man would not be able to love his people as he loved them. He believed a younger man would no doubt have the energy and the vision and the zeal to take the church to new heights, but he worried about a younger man loving the people.

When I became the pastor, I did not expect to have the love capacity that Dr. Jack Hyles possessed, but I did expect God to be the same source of love as my predecessor knew. I believed that God could love Brother Hyles' people through me.

First Baptist Church has grown, and I believe the people do feel loved. We have continued to say as a church to the community, "We are still here to love you." We have continued to say to the fallen, the poor, and the lost, "We are still here to love you." We have said to the world, "We love you more than we have ever loved you."

The fear of leadership is always "Will the next person be able to love with the kind of love I demonstrated? Will my children love their children to the same degree, with the same compassion, the same empowerment, and with the same partnership that I would want them to have if I were the parents?"

Jesus faced this same fear. When He left the earth, He Who is love had to leave all of His converts in the hands of His disciples. How could those mere human beings tell them how much Jesus loved them? But do you know what? They did!

Leadership needs to possess confidence, patience, and understanding; but leadership especially must have the ability to communicate love. Happy followers are those who feel cared for and loved. Allow me to practically demonstrate the language of servant leadership in three practical areas: marriage, parenting, and the employer-employee relationship.

MARRIAGE

Languages for both the husband and the wife are present in every servant-leader marriage relationship. Know to what languages your spouse responds! Is it the language of understanding, or of patience, or of personality? The humorist Dave Barry quipped:

What women want: To be loved, to be listened to, to be desired, to be respected, to be needed, to be trusted, and sometimes, just to be held. What men want: Tickets for the World Series.[3]

With that humorous illustration so aptly describing the different languages of men and women, let me acquaint you with just a few of these husband and wife languages.

1. **The language of listening.** In so many marriages I find there is an absolute failure on the part of the husband and the wife to listen to each other.

People everywhere love to be listened to, and they almost always respond to others who listen to them. Listening is one of the best techniques we have for showing respect to someone else. It's an indication that we consider them important human beings.[4]

2. **The language of words.** Many a wife responds very powerfully to the romantic words or words of affection from her husband. However, many husbands do not understand the importance of this particular language. When this couple seeks marriage counseling, it is not because of affairs or bankruptcy or other troubles, it is totally because the husband does not use the words that would make his wife feel loved. On the other hand, a husband may be very moved by words, and his wife simply will not give him those needed words of trust and affection.

For those who want a relationship to continue: Communicate. Negotiate. Compromise. You must be able and willing to change. You must be able to consider another person's needs. You must talk with each other, not just guess what your partner is thinking. What else are words for?[5]

One very important love language of the servant-leader relationship is words. The power of words was reaffirmed to me when I came across the following incredible illustration in the book *21 Days to a Great Marriage.*

> Several years ago *Reader's Digest* printed the story of a remarkable junior high teacher at St. Mary's School in Morris, Minnesota. One Friday afternoon this teacher asked her students to make a list of the names of all the other students in the class. Then she told them to write down, beside each name, the nicest thing they could say about each of their classmates. At the end of the period she collected the sheets. Then, over the weekend she made a separate sheet for each student, and on that sheet she listed all the things that had been said about each person by his or her classmates. On Monday she gave each student his or her list.

> As the kids began reading, they started whispering to each other. "I never knew you thought that about me." "I didn't know others liked me so much." The papers were never discussed in the class, but the teacher knew the exercise was a success because she could see the difference

this positive feedback made in the students' attitudes about themselves.

Several years later one of the students, Mark Ekland, was killed in Vietnam. After his body was returned to Minnesota, most of his classmates, as well as the math teacher, attended the funeral. At the luncheon after the service, Mark's father approached the teacher and said, "They found this on Mark when he was killed. We thought you might recognize it." He handed her two worn sheets of notebook paper that had been taped, and refolded many times. It was the list of good things Mark's classmates had written about him.

"Thank you so much for doing that," Mark's father told the teacher. "As you can see, our son treasured it." Several of Mark's classmates had been standing nearby and overheard this conversation. One by one they began to reveal that each of them still carried his or her sheet of comments and read it often. Some carried it in a billfold: one had even put it in his wedding album.

One young man said, "I think we all saved our list."

That's the power of affirming, encouraging words.

Do you think your wife has a list like that tucked away somewhere in her mind? Are you noticing, appreciating, and verbalizing the nicest things you can say about your wife?

"You are the man," right? Then show your wife, in word and in deed, some encouragement each and every day, and I guarantee you'll not only hear that phrase from her often (in her own way, of course), but she'll do all she can to make you feel that you *are* the man![6]

3.   The Language of Time. Do you really want your wife to think that she is not important when she calls the office and the message she is given is "Tell my wife that I don't have time to talk to her now"? What statement is that husband making? It is not the language of love.

Some time ago a psychologist ran an experiment measuring the amount of conversation that occurs between the average wife and husband in a week's time. To make the experiment accurate, the researcher strapped portable electronic microphones to the subjects and measured every word they uttered–idle conversation while driving to the store, requests to pass the toast, everything.

There are 168 hours in a week, 10,080 minutes. How much of that time do you suppose the average couple devotes to talking to each other? No, not 10 hours, not a single hour, or even 30 minutes. The conversation took, on the average, a grand total of 17 minutes. "Loneliness," says Germaine Greer, "is never more cruel that when it is felt in close propinquity with someone who has ceased to communicate."[7]

We simply must make time for people! Remember when Jesus was on His way to heal Jairus' daughter and a woman touched Him? A large crowd of perhaps 10,000 to 20,000 people were thronging Jesus. They all wanted to touch Him, and Jesus was instantly aware that someone had touched Him.

Jesus knew the person who had touched Him desperately needed Him. He took the time to stop in His mission for one woman. Giving one's time is a powerful demonstration of the language of love.

4.   The Language of Presence. Wife, may I share a powerful secret about your husband? He likes you to be near him. I have a great neighbor, and I have noticed this couple knows how to have a happy marriage. When he mows the lawn, she sits on the deck and just watches him mow the lawn. Why? A man loves to be watched—especially by his wife.

Wife, if you don't want to watch the ball game with your husband, you can read a book as you sit by him, at the very least. A husband likes his wife to be with him, and many women don't understand that language of love. He doesn't care to talk; he just feels tremendous love when his wife says, "I will sit here and watch you clean your guns." He doesn't want or need her help to clean his guns! She doesn't need to participate. Her presence is yet another language of love.

If you want to help another person, just be there. Your presence does wonders. If you want to help another person, just listen. One of the greatest gifts one person can give to another is the gift of listening. It can be an act of love and caring. But far too many people in conversations only *hear* one another. Few actually *listen*.[8]

5.   The Language of Touch. Most ladies understand intimately the language of touch. As two ladies talk and commune with each other, they often reach out to each other and touch one another's hand or the forearm. Touching is bonding.

> We talk to each other with smiles, with handshakes, with hugs, with laughter, with eye contact, with touching, holding, enfolding, and a myriad of gestures. These, too, are languages—some of which may "speak louder than words."[9]

Many a man does not understand that his wife likes to be touched.

6. The Language of Completing Tasks. Husband, remember that list of "to-dos" your wife asked you to complete 17 years ago? The gutter is still not on. The cabinet still isn't painted; in fact, it's too late to paint the cabinet. She gave up and sold it three years ago at a garage sale! That list just seems to collect more dust. A wife feels so loved when her husband tells her to make her list, and he says, "I will do three of these chores today, one tomorrow, and the rest will be completed in two weeks." In her mind she might say, "Sure…like always," but when the tasks are completed in two weeks as promised, she feels incredibly loved.

What language speaks volumes to your spouse? Protection? Romance? Material needs? Most men only perfect one way in which to express their love. The other way they most often choose is nonchalantly handing out money, but truthfully, most of the time, money is not the best language of love. Having tasks completed or talking often means more to a wife than having money. A wise servant-leader husband learns the language of his wife, and a wise servant-leader wife learns the language of her husband. Each must ask and answer the question, "To what does my spouse most respond?"

PARENTING

The challenge of the servant-leader parent is to change languages as the child matures. I have already mentioned that a teenager does not respond well to the language of a child. What are some of the love languages of a child? Playtime, coloring, being read to, cuddling, and stroking are several languages to which children respond. Just try any of these with a teenager! Language changes, and the servant leader has to understand the change of language.

1.   The Language of Participation. The child responds to the language of participation by saying, "Mommy, can I help you do that?" It doesn't matter what task you are doing; a child believes he can do anything, and he wants to do it **with** you. That need to participate is why toy manufacturers make miniature plastic lawn mowers. About the time you have trained the boy that he can do it alone and you want to trade mowers with him, he doesn't care to participate anymore! Pushing a mower or working with Dad is a language of love. The foolish father who is not a servant leader says, "I will take care of the lawn myself."

Some dads excuse their lack of participation by saying, "I am not the loving kind of dad." Showing a language of love doesn't mean you have to say "I love you." My father wasn't the kind of man who said "I love you" to me, but Dad did other things. Dad's idea of loving me was saying, "Jake, come here; give me a hand with this toolbox." I carried the toolbox with him; he carried 99 percent of the weight, and I carried the other part.

I remember once trying to help him carry a ten-foot section of three-inch galvanized pipe. He was going to swing the pipe over a three-foot-wide ditch. I stumbled, so he picked up the pipe and me and swung us both over the ditch. He said, "Son, am I glad you were on the other end of that pipe!"

"Yeah," I responded, "I like helping you."

I was too naive to realize that I really wasn't much of a help to my dad. My dad used great wisdom in showing the love language of letting a little boy participate in his work.

There is a stage where a little girl likes to help Mom. "I want to help you cook, Mom!" she exclaims. She thinks licking the beaters is helping her mother! The truth is, probably a child helping in the kitchen isn't doing much more than creating a big mess, but participating in her mother's work is the language of love. When the child asks to help, too many mothers say, "Not now, I am too busy. You run along." Those words say, "I don't love you."

The fundamental complaint of young Americans… does not refer to the hypocrisies, lies, errors, blunders and problems they have inherited. It is, instead, this: That they cannot talk with grown people.…I have come to believe that the great majority of our kids have never enjoyed an intimate friendship with even one grown person. Why not? When you ask that you get one answer: Their efforts to communicate with us are invariably and completely squelched.[10]

Saying "I love you" is only one part of the language of love. How many times does Jesus say "I love you" in the New Testament? If you are looking for those exact words, you will not find them very many times at all. He proved His love in the love language we can understand—the Cross. He chose a language mankind could understand.

2. The Language of Attention. Every child wants his parents to watch him when he learns to ride a bike. "Dad! Mom! Watch me! No hands!" Jack Canfield, the inspirational speaker and writer, says, "The greatest deficit in America is the attention deficit of our children. The average child gets 14 minutes of attention a day from each of his parents. The greatest thing we can give a kid is time."

3. The Language of Questioning. The love language of a child is "Why?" There is a zone of life in parenting when parents may feel like they are nothing more than a walking dictionary. The wisest answer is "Father Encyclopedia is here; let me share with you from the fountain of knowledge!" Trust me; the day will come when no more questions will be asked because they reach 13, and suddenly they have all the answers!

4. The Language of Role Playing. Children love to act out situations. They love to role play the right way and the wrong way. All they need is an audience.

WHAT ARE THE LOVE LANGUAGES OF TEENAGERS?

1. The Language of Distant Presence. Teenagers hate coming home to an empty house, but neither do they want to be smothered when they walk in the door. They want to open the door, smell something cooking, and know that Mom has been home working. If he says, "Mom, I'm home," he really doesn't want an answer; he is making a statement. He wants you—at a distance. Teenagers want you to go their games, but they want a distant presence. They want to be able to spot you and know that you came, but don't get any closer.

2. The Language of Independence. A wise servant-leader father says to his child, "I'm going to the store, might get an ice cream cone afterward, want to go along?" Try saying that to your 16-year old! He'll say, "Give me the car keys, and I will go for you." He desires independence. The wise servant-leader parents realize that, so they don't try to treat the teenager like a child.

3. The Language of Trust. "The teen years can be a tough time for the parent-child relationship. Teens often want a lot of autonomy but do not yet have the life experience needed to make good decisions. Teens want to be trusted. Parents can't help but worry."[11]

4. The Language of Risk Taking. What do you do when your son says, "Come on, Dad! Try the snowboard!" You try, and be sure the spectators have the name of your doctor in case you pass out on the way down!

5. The Language of Friends. A wise parent doesn't

compete with his teenager's friends; he works with them. "Friendship reflects a deep regard for the value of the person. In a friendship, each individual affirms the other's presence and reinforces the other's integrity."[12] Wise servant-leader parents recognize their teen's need for friends.

6. The Language of Music and Media. Provide an avenue for them to enjoy the right kind of music.

7. The Language of Being a Spectator. The following dialogue explains how being a spectator shows love.

"Dad, are you working late tonight?"

"No, Son. What do you need?"

"I just have a big game, and I didn't know if you were coming or not."

"Sure, I'll be there."

That assurance is all they want to hear. They don't want you to come and take lots of pictures. They don't want you to coach them or the game from sidelines. They don't want to be yelled at. They don't want to be coddled. They want to get in the car after the game, and they want you to say, "That was a great game. You played well." That is all a parent has to say. Then add, "Let's get some pizza!" They will love you forever, especially if you say, "Invite three of your friends to come along."

8. The Language of Participation. "Do it with me." For instance, teenagers don't want to cook with their parents; that is what a child says. But teenagers do like to have their parents watch them perform.

9. The Language of Understanding. "Understanding

occurs on two levels: *Emotionally*—the person feels that you understand what they are feeling—and *intellectually*—the person believes that you understand what they are saying."[13] Teens desperately want to be heard, to be understood, and to be loved.

10. The Language of Clear Guidelines. Don't confuse your teenagers. Make a few, simple rules for them to follow. A teen may gripe the whole time he follows the guidelines, but he wants them.

These are just a few of the many languages of love for a teenager. Learn what languages move your teen.

EMPLOYER-EMPLOYEE RELATIONSHIPS

An incomplete list of the languages of love for a servant-leader employer to employee include the following:

1. The Language of Trust. Someone has said that trust is the glue that binds followers and leaders together. "Trust implies accountability, predictability, and reliability. More than anything else, followers want to believe in and trust their leaders."[14] They also want the trust of their leader.

2. The Language of Empowerment. "At the core of leadership is guiding and empowering those we lead. When we do so with skill, love, and grace, the effects radiate far beyond those we personally touch."[15]

3. The Language of Responsibility. Ken Blanchard said, "The best way to develop responsibility in people is to give them responsibility."[16]

4. The Language of Private Correction. "Leaders praise in public, and admonish in private."[17]

5. The Language of Public Praise. In his book *How to Be a Better Leader*, Rupert Eales-White asserted, "A single word of praise has more motivational power than a thousand words of blame."[18]

6. The Language of Recognition. The successful businesswoman who founded the Mary Kay empire, Mary Kay Ash, has said, "Everyone has an invisible sign hanging from his neck saying, 'Make me feel important!' Never forget this message when working with people."[19] People need to be recognized for their merit with their leader's reassurance and regular encouragement.

Reward, recognition, praise. It doesn't matter how you do it; what matters is that you do it, again and again and again. The bottom line on rewarding employees is this. Sure, money's wonderful. But it's not the only effective reward. If you have money to spend, use it intelligently. Reward excellence.

And follow the advice of writer and lecturer Florence Littauer, [who] was asked unexpectedly one day to teach the children at her church. One passage from Ephesians came to mind, but it was a difficult one for the children to grasp: *"Let no corrupt communication proceed out of your mouth, but that which is good to the use of edifying, that it may minister grace unto the hearers."* (Ephesians 4:29)

Littauer worked with the children, deciphering the

difficult words, and finally came up with an interpretation that she felt captured the meaning of the passage: "Our words really should be like a present," she said, and the children seemed to agree. "A little gift. Something that we give to other people. Something that they want. Something that they reach out for. They grab our words, and they take them in, and they love them. Because our words made them feel so good."

Littauer went on like that a bit, comparing words to gifts. Then she summed up her message. "Now," she said, "let's start from the beginning. My words should not be bad. They should be good. They should be used to build up, not knock down. They should be words that would come out like a present."

When she finished, a little girl jumped up and said in a loud and clear voice, "What she means is," and then the girl stopped to catch her breath. "What she means is that our words should be like a little silver box with a bow on top."

Praise is not only welcomed by children. It goes a long way in the business world as well.[20]

7. The Language of Personal Family Awareness. Employees like it when the boss asks, "How is your daughter doing?" "How is her boyfriend getting along with her?" "How is your son doing with his bout with the flu?"

"People don't care how much you know until they know how much you care...about them."[21] Employees don't care if you socialize with them; they just want to know you are aware they have a family. General Omar Bradley wrote,

> A leader should possess human understanding and consideration for others. People are not robots and should not be treated as such. I do not by any means suggest coddling. But people are intelligent, complicated beings who will respond favorably to human understanding and consideration. By these means their leader will get maximum effort from each of them. He will also get loyalty.[22]

8. The Language of Concern. "A friend of mine characterizes leaders simply like this: 'Leaders don't inflict pain; they bear pain.' "[23]

9. The Language of Fairness. God doesn't deal in fairness; He deals in compensation.

> Leading at a higher level is a process defined *as the process of achieving worthwhile results while acting with respect, care, and fairness for the well-being of all involved.* When that occurs, self-serving leadership is not possible. Why? Self-serving leaders think that leadership is all about them and not about the interests of those they serve. Robert Greenleaf said, "Serve first and lead second."[24]

10. The Language of Challenge. I find that I must pull and stretch my people to do more than they think they are capable of to develop and challenge them to greater works. Henry Kissinger described a leader as "an individual who created an alchemy of vision that moved people from where they were to places that they have never been before."[25]

11. The Language of Discretionary Time. Occasionally give an employee a day off, and he will love you.

The desire for the different languages of love never goes away from childhood to teenager to adult. The sooner one learns the language of leadership, the sooner he becomes a powerful servant leader.

Jesus was the expert at displaying servant leadership. Luke 8:40 says, *"And it came to pass, that, when Jesus was returned, the people gladly received him: for they were all waiting for him."* Crowds gathered everywhere to see and hear Jesus because He spoke a language that every man, woman, and child understood. The person who wants to reach the multitudes must learn the language of the multitudes. The difficulty is learning yet another language. The challenge of the servant leader is that he must learn all the languages so he can be effective. The language everyone understands is the language of love.

> Leadership is not about love—it *is* love. It is loving your mission, it is loving your people, and it is loving yourself enough to get out of the way so other people can be magnificent."[26]

10

"Setting an example is not the main means of influencing another. It is the means."
— Albert Schweitzer

MAKING YOUR FOLLOWERS

"My brethren, be not many masters, knowing that we shall receive the greater condemnation." (James 3:1)

This verse was penned by a pastor, who is wisely addressing the issue of leadership. James, the outspoken half-brother of Christ, under the inspiration of the Holy Ghost, is saying a man should be careful about desiring to be a leader because he will be judged by a greater number of people on a broader spectrum. He will also be judged more harshly by just about everyone who believes he has the right to tell the leader how to lead! In this chapter, I would like to address one of the weaker areas of Biblical leadership.

I believe the most difficult phase of servant leadership is the servant part. I really don't mind being a leader, and I don't mind the buck stopping at me, so to speak. However, as soon as I must address the problems my leadership generates, then leadership no longer becomes fun.

A leader is not simply born. "The 'natural-born leader' is a myth. Certainly, there may be a small element of leadership that is intangible, but leadership is an art and science that can be learned."[1] I personally believe leadership is a spiritual gift given by God. As far as leading and daring to take charge, many people have some natural gifts in that area. Unfortunately, some people think they are leaders who are not. That scenario becomes doubly a problem when these leaders who are not leaders are also not servant leaders. Those people just enjoy giving orders.

Others lead by example, and that is a good method, but a lot of leadership is not example. A lot of leadership involves the other side which is servant leadership, and the servant leader handles the problems created by the example leaders.

Therefore, I want to look at the portion of servant leadership which James addresses. Servant leadership is not just about saying, "Follow me, and we will do something big."

1.   God gives the ability to lead to certain men. God calls men, and according to Romans 11:29 which says, *"...the gifts and calling of God are without repentance,"* when He calls, He gifts a man. God called men like Abraham, Moses, Joshua,

David, and many others to lead. Sometimes God gives a man leadership, and when He calls that man, sometimes that man doesn't yield to God's call. In these cases, we see very gifted leaders forging ahead in the business world or other such realms of influence where perhaps God didn't necessarily ask them to lead. God had gifted this leader for another work.

I have met men in the business world and have actually said to them, "You should have been a preacher." Some of them have even admitted that they considered that avenue when they were younger. By their own admission, they stated, "I forgot about it, or I didn't recognize it as God's calling."

Many people are gifted by God with leadership, but they don't understand the call of God and never use the gift in the service of God. But God never changes His mind because the gifts and calling of God are without repentance. God never changes His mind about the gifts He gives to us and never changes His mind about how He intended for us to use those gifts.

2. Leadership is like horsepower—the more you have, the more difficult it is to control it. In our neighborhood I noticed a boy on a moped wearing a racer's motorcycle outfit, complete with helmet, boots, and leather gloves. When he cranked the throttle on that moped, he could maybe muster 9 horsepower. I thought, "Does he know exactly how uncool he is?"

Another person in our neighborhood must have agreed with how I felt because he too had noticed this boy on his moped. This man, who hasn't grown up totally, has a tricked-out a 200-pound motocross bike that is about 450 cc cranking about 90 horsepower. The power to weight ratio is excessive. When he comes out wearing his gear and fires up that screaming machine, I can smell the Castrol mix.

When he sees the moped rider, he roars from his garage with his back tire standing up, holding one throttle, while waving at the kid. As I have watched, I have to admit I thought, "That is so cool!" That motocross bike had a lot more horsepower than that little moped did, and that adult rider who thought he was still a teenager had to be careful how he controlled that power.

Leadership works in much the same way. Some leaders are phenomenal leaders in their ability to get people to follow them. Military leaders are representative of this type of phenomenal leadership.

The most famous examples of military leadership arise in situations where the leader spurs his under-armed and bedraggled followers on their last legs and with no ammunition left, to great feats of valor. Winston Churchill's greatest moments came when London was being bombed and an invasion of England seemed imminent. Leaders…are individuals who made ordinary people do extraordinary things in the face of adversity.[2]

The greater the leadership ability, the more "horsepower." The wise servant leader knows what he is facing before kicking in the horsepower. He realizes his leadership could create more problems than he is capable of handling. Servant leadership is all about handling the peripheral problems that develop from raw leadership.

The Bible does not place emphasis on Moses' great leadership ability; rather, it emphasizes the great quality of meekness which characterized Moses. *Meekness* is "his ability to control his leadership." Moses had to learn meekness because the area that the Bible first emphasized about Moses was his mouth. In Exodus 2 Moses killed an Egyptian; he exerted his leadership without thought of the peripheral damage. *"And when he went out the second day, behold, two men of the Hebrews strove together: and he said to him that did the wrong, Wherefore smitest thou thy fellow? And he said, Who made thee a prince and a judge over us? intendest thou to kill me, as thou killedst the Egyptian? And Moses feared, and said, Surely this thing is known."* (Exodus 2:13, 14) Moses had no trouble taking the bull by the horns! But when he tried to be a peacemaker, he was confronted with his sin!

In Exodus 3 a humbled Moses who has been living in the desert sees the burning bush and accepts the call of God. *"And Moses said unto the LORD, O my Lord, I am not eloquent, neither heretofore, nor since thou hast spoken unto thy servant: but I am slow of speech, and of a slow tongue."* (Exodus 4:10) What a pitiful excuse! Moses possessed a quick tongue! He had been educated in the finest of schools! Moses was a phenomenal leader, and leadership almost always gets in trouble with the tongue.

Leaders always know what to do. They have an opinion about everything. Many a strong leader has great difficulty in admitting, "I don't know" because he **does** know. When a strong leader says, "I don't know," that answer usually means he doesn't want to say what he is thinking because he needs to consider the situation a little longer before he speaks. That lesson is what Moses had to learn.

Though he claimed to be slow of speech and have a slow tongue, he still acted in haste when he called the Hebrews rebellious, and he smote the rock twice. Moses forfeited his opportunity to enter the Promised Land. His mouth got him into trouble, and at times his mouth got him out of trouble.

Strong leadership has an uncanny ability to form quick opinions and make snap decisions. Good leadership is the ability to form quick comparisons, evaluations, and analyses. Good leadership sizes up people very quickly. Good leadership understands great principles.

Raw leadership knows, "I don't have to be right, but I have to decide." Many people cannot lead because they cannot make the decision. When questioned about whether or not it is the right decision, good leadership never falters, is never afraid to make the needed decision, and is never worried about being wrong.

Too many people are so careful they even want to micromanage the damage control. Before they can make a decision, they begin formulating a series of questions to ask about the situation. Soon it is too late to make the decision! Good leaders have to decide. For some, it is a gift given to them by God.

A servant-leader doesn't worry about some wrong decisions because that decision-making ability is a gift from God. Where true servant leadership shines is in all of the residual fallout that comes from those snap decisions that were made when a decision had to be made; some of them were wrong, and some people were hurt because of it.

I make an average of 700 decisions a week in this ministry. I am talking about official decisions that the staff would ask me or that the ministry require me to make. I don't have time to think about every one of them. If I averaged spending ten minutes thinking over each question, that is a thousand minutes. I don't have that many minutes in a day! I know that I must stay prayed up! I must possess the mind of Christ.

3. Leadership is a gift from God that attracts followers, but the key is leading people without hurting them. The world is filled with fairly good leaders who can take people somewhere. However, leadership is not simply taking one's followers to a greater destination; it is making them into greater individuals. The greatest verse and the greatest statement in the world about leadership can be found in Matthew 4:19: *"And he saith unto them, Follow me, and I will make you fishers of men."* Servant leadership is epitomized by the Lord Jesus Christ. Leadership answers, "What can I become if I follow you?"

Raw leadership says, "Follow me, and I will take you *somewhere*." Servant leadership says, "If you follow me, I will make something of you." That principle is the key emphasis in the Word of God on leadership.

So much of leadership is concerned with a leader's ability to attract followers and his creating an appetite for people to follow him.

The signs of outstanding leadership appear primarily among the followers. Are the followers reaching their potential? Are they learning? Serving? Do they achieve the required results? Do they change with grace? Manage conflict?[3]

Servant leadership possesses dedication, humility, drive, compassion, creativity, energy, zeal, good health, imagination, and yes, if you follow Jesus, you will be the one who will become something different! Servant leadership emphasizes what the follower will become—not where the leader is taking them. "Inspiring and challenging others and watching them rise to their full potential is the complex, yet enormously, rewarding role of the leader."[4] The greatest of leaders wrap themselves therefore in a servant's garment. With so many strong leaders, whether a military leader or a business leader, there is a distance between the leader and follower because their central premise of leadership method is all about "Follow *me*." That is raw leadership—not servant leadership.

The late Robert Greenleaf, a former AT&T executive, is well known for his concept of leaders as servants of the people. He advocates service to others as the leaders' primary purpose. If people feel you are genuinely interested in serving others, then they will be prepared not just to follow you but to dedicate themselves to the common cause.[5]

The greatness of Dr. Jack Hyles was that he took his people

somewhere, and as he took them, he made them into something greater. Servant leadership is approachable.

THE WISDOM OF THE SERVANT LEADER

"Who is a wise man and endued with knowledge among you? let him shew out of a good conversation his works with meekness of wisdom. But if ye have bitter envying and strife in your hearts, glory not, [Don't flaunt it] *and lie not against the truth. This wisdom descendeth not from above, but is earthly, sensual, devilish. For where envying and strife is, there is confusion and every evil work. But the wisdom that is from above is first pure, then peaceable...."* (James 3:13-17)

1. **Pure Wisdom.** James says that a man who wants to be a leader needs pure wisdom. The word *pure* or *purity* has several definitions in reference to leadership.

- *Purity* means "modesty." That definition seldom describes leadership. Being modest doesn't fit in with the context of what most leaders believe is leadership. A strong servant leader does not have to have his way. Jesus' style of leadership was meekness.
- *Purity* means "clean"—morally pure and clean.
- *Purity* means "immaculate." Servant leadership is not sloppy or dirty leadership. It is not lazy or unkempt leadership. It is fastidious. The immaculate servant leader says, "Everything under my care is important."
- *Purity* means "perfect." The word *perfect* means "mature."

2. Peaceable Wisdom. The word *peaceable* in James 3:17 means "loving peace." The servant leader loves to bring peace to every situation. Trying to bring peace sometimes means trying unbelievable solutions to have that peace. A Bible servant leader brings peace into every setting and zone for which he is responsible while pushing his followers forward and patting them on the back. Harvey S. Firestone, the founder of Firestone Tires, said, "The growth and development of people is the highest calling of leadership."[6]

The true servant leader lives to one day hear the words, "Well done, thou good and faithful servant!" "True servant leadership embraces a humble sincerity that brings out the best in leaders and in those they serve."[7]

When we think of success or greatness, we think of giving commands and being obeyed. When we think of greatness, we think of having much. When Jesus thought of greatness, He thought of giving much. When we think of greatness, we think of being served. When Jesus thought of greatness, He thought of serving."

– Dr. Jack Hyles[8]

"When we are out of sympathy with the young,
then I think our work in this world is over."
– George MacDonald

WHAT I DREAM
FOR OUR CHILDREN

"I will sing a new song unto thee, O God: upon a psaltery and an instrument of ten strings will I sing praises unto thee. It is he that giveth salvation unto kings: who delivereth David his servant from the hurtful sword. Rid me, and deliver me from the hand of strange children, whose mouth speaketh vanity, and their right hand is a right hand of falsehood: That our sons may be as plants grown up in their youth; that our daughters may be as corner stones, polished after the similitude of a palace: That our garners may be full, *affording all manner of store: that our sheep may bring forth thousands and ten thousands in our streets: That our oxen may be strong to labour; that there be no breaking in, nor going out; that there be no complaining in our streets. Happy is that people, that is in such a case: yea, happy is that people, whose God is the LORD."* (Psalm 144:9-15)

1. I dream they would know the security and stability of parents who stay together. *"It is he that giveth salvation unto kings: who delivereth David his servant from the hurtful sword."* (Psalm 144:10) I do not know of one single thing that will do more to help the next generation develop a stable and secure emotional structure, spiritual structure, social structure, and a solid mental framework than for parents to stay together.

Researchers—both Christian and secular—agree that the single most damaging thing that has happened in our society to children is the breakup of the home. Some people believe it would be better for children to have divorced parents getting along reasonably from a distance than sitting in their home and enduring all of the feuding. My answer for that excuse is to stop the arguing and stay married! Only selfish parents lack the character to stay together. The option of divorce is a shallow choice. "Every choice we make, whether it is good or bad, has consequences."[1] Divorce has unending consequences.

If President Bill Clinton was able to persuade Yasir Arafat of the Palestinian Liberation Organization and the Prime Minister of Israel, who hate each other, to sit down together, eat a meal together, pose together for a photo op, and agree to peace terms, then surely a husband and a wife can sit down together, stop fighting, and behave themselves! Decide to get along! I realize that problems and disagreements arise that bring strife into a home sometimes. That strife is not the issue. The important issue is there has to be a better way to reconcile for your children's sake than simply saying, "Your father and I have come to the point that we can't live with each other." The signal being sent to those kids is that God isn't big enough and what the Bible says does not matter.

Moms and Dads on the road to parenting, build a home where you plan to stay together! My dream is for every boy and girl to be able to say, "I grew up in a home where my parents dealt with some tension, but they told us that they were always staying together. They loved each other, and they loved God. They loved us children enough to show us that there was always a way to make their marriage work."

Parents, show your kids that the Bible contains some answers. Show your kids that the God to Whom you pray can come through. God may not take away all the problems; in fact, I seriously doubt that God will take away a good percentage of the problems. God will only take away a sufficient amount for you to survive because God wants you to live on grace—not your spouse's goodness. God wants you to learn the qualities of mercy and forgiveness.

King David endured terrible times when his son rebelled against him, when he had an affair with Bath-sheba, and when he felt the kingdom would be taken from him. God forgave David for his indiscretions, but his family paid a heavy price for David's sins. The bottom line is that David realized he had made a tragic mistake, and he and Bath-sheba stayed together. David's problems did not go away, but he maintained his integrity through the whole debacle.

You get in trouble. Your spouse has a breach of character and was unethical or improper, or worse, immoral. Don't make the first phone call to the lawyer; make your first phone call to the preacher. Find someone who knows how to get a hold of God.

2.   I dream that our children would have a happy mother and a happy father who enjoy life. *"That our oxen may be strong to labour; that there be no breaking in, nor going out; that there be no complaining in our streets."* (Psalm 144:14) Our children need to be surrounded with adults who enjoy loving and serving God.

I know the people who live next door to us say, "Our neighbors are the weirdest people in the world—they go to church every day of the week. They go to church all day on Sunday; they spend all day bus calling on Saturday, and they give away all their money. I don't understand it—they don't have nearly what we have, but they surely are happy."

Do you want happy kids? Show them a happy marriage. The best thing a dad can do for his children is to love their mother. The very best thing a mother can do for her children is to love their father.

By the way, if divorce has invaded your home and you have remarried, the worst thing you can do to your children is to be antagonistic toward your ex-spouse. Antagonism does nothing good for children, especially when selfish parents try to win their children's approval by spitting venom about each other and blaming each other for the divorce. The blood tie will never be severed.

If an ex-spouse is living a wayward, disappointing life, let the children see that for themselves. James 3:10 says, *"Out of the same mouth proceedeth blessing and cursing. My brethren, these things ought not so to be."* The stronger spouse says to the children, "I want you to love your father (mother)." What you teach that you don't teach is more powerful than what you teach by teaching. It is what you say that you don't say. It is what comes out of your mouth that wasn't part of the lesson plan. Bible Christianity is giving our children happy homes.

In reading and studying for this book, I read about an insurance executive who had a staff of about 25 people, and he noticed his sales were declining. He contacted consultants, read books, and applied different methodology, but nothing seemed to push the reset button. One day he went to work early and merely observed his employees as they arrived at work. He called a meeting and stated, "Effective immediately, you will come to work beginning tomorrow with a smile on your face and with a happy spirit, or you will be fired." The reset button was pushed, and sales went up 35% the next month. He noticed that when his employees arrived, they greeted each other with negative talk—bad marriage, bad traffic, bad weather, bad month for sales, etc. What a horribly contagious attitude!

In his book *Top Performance: How to Develop Excellence in Yourself and Others*, Zig Ziglar said, "Happiness is not a where or a when, it is a here or a now."[2] Just by listening and observing, this insurance executive discovered what methodology and consultants could not ascertain. "No one can possibly know everything. Listening to others is the single best way to learn."[3] Happy spirits are contagious.

3.   I dream that our young people and children would be allowed to ripen in the same place they were planted. *"That our sons may be as plants grown up in their youth; that our daughters may be as corner stones, polished after the similitude of a palace."* (Psalm 144:12) One of the best places to plant them is in a good church with a good Sunday school program and bus routes and youth activities and camps and music groups. Plant them in a good Christian school where they will receive good training. By the time they reach adulthood, they will be properly ripened for the work of God.

Keep in mind that high school young people are not ripened when they graduate. One of the most fragile times in life is when a teenager graduates from high school. He is not yet polished, and God's desire is for him to be polished in the place where he was chosen or ripened in the place where he was planted.

A couple of older teenagers will sometimes come to me declaring their undying love for one another. One such couple whom I will call Tom and Mary came to see me. I knew what they expected to hear from me. I said, "I am not going to give you a lecture. I want to ask you a question. Do you know anything about computers?"

"I love computers," Tom eagerly replied.

"You probably know more about computers than I do. Have you ever loaded any software programs on your computer?" I asked.

"All the time!"

"You know how that little bar comes up and starts saying what percentage of software is loaded," I said. "It goes really fast through 5%, 10%, 15%, 20%…and all of a sudden it gets to about 95%, then slows way down and hangs at 99% while you wait and wait and wait. Why is it taking so long? Do you know what it is doing during that last little bit?"

"Oh, that's easy," he said, "At that point the program is basically loaded on your machine, but it is integrating with the whole system so it can talk with the whole computer."

"Exactly," I said. "The first 99% was just information loaded on your hard drive, but now it has to insert the smart keys, add the symbols to the opening page, prepare the access, and how to input moves. What would happen if you shut off the machine at 99% and came back tomorrow? How much of that software program would you be able to play?"

"Zero," Tom said.

"Tom, you are 99% loaded, but you need that other 1%. Truthfully, that 1% is the most important 1% of all the hundred. You need to get integrated to take everything you have learned from the time you were a little tiny toddler and how to make all that you learned through these 18 years functional in adulthood. As your pastor, I still need to teach you to take what you have already learned and transfer it to a young boy who will someday call you daddy. We need to teach you,

Mary, how to transfer all of the love and affection you feel for Tom to your daughter who will someday love a husband. Your parents, your teachers, and I, as your pastor, need a couple more years with you."

Tom looked at me and said, "That makes a lot of sense to me."

Mary looked at me and said, "You mean we can't get married?"

I loved what happened next! Before I could answer, Tom looked at her and said, "Duh, yeah. I got to load. I got to get integrated."

I thought, "This kid is good! Then I said, "Tom, can I hire you just to be my translator for all the teens who don't get what you understood so easily!"

Teenagers need that last 1%! It isn't just enough to read or go to school or earn a piece of paper that acknowledges so many credit hours of sitting in a classroom enduring Christian school teachers. Every teenager needs to ripen. Ripening involves being around other adults who have already become what he needs to become.

Polishing is the application of something that can grind on you. One isn't polished by just wishing he were bright and shiny. To be polished, one must go to a place of polishing and ripening and welcome that polishing and ripening.

4.   **I dream that our children would clearly see the line between the perverse and the pure.** "*…rid me, and deliver me out of great waters, from the hand of strange children; Whose mouth speaketh vanity, and their right hand is a right hand of false-*

hood....Rid me, and deliver me from the hand of strange children, whose mouth speaketh vanity, and their right hand is a right hand of falsehood." (Psalm 144:7, 8, 11) I believe the Psalmist is saying that a very clear line needs to be established between the perverse or the wicked and the pure.

When I was the captain of an East Chicago bus route, I often took our children, Kenny and Jaclynn, with me every week to visit. I kept them out until they started asking, "Are we going home soon, Dad?" As soon as I heard those words, I always said, "Yes, I am going home right now." I never said, "No, we are going to stay here and visit three more hours whether or not you like it." I never wanted them to get a bad taste about serving God. Oftentimes we would stop at Dairy Queen or Munster Gyros on the way home and get some food. We had a lot of fun together.

As we were leaving East Chicago one day, I noticed Jaclynn staring at a big billboard sign advertising liquor with an immodestly dressed couple standing seductively close. As soon as we passed the sign, she turned and looked back at it. On the reverse side was an ad for an insurance company. She was very quiet, and I asked, "Jaclynn, what are you looking at?"

"Dad, why don't they ever show the other side of the billboard?"

"I don't know, sweetheart." I knew what she meant because we had just visited some of the homes of the children who rode on our church bus. At one home in particular, a little girl who came every week ran out to see us. Her drunken dad followed her, and he began cursing at us. He finally left, and through the open door, I could see the heartbroken mother dissolving in tears on the sofa. She kept asking, "What am I going to do? What a miserable, wretched life we have!" Beer bottles were strewn throughout the house, and the stench of liquor permeated the filthy place.

Yes, I immediately knew what Jaclynn meant when she solemnly asked, "Why don't they show the other side of the billboard, Daddy?" But, they never do, do they?

Sad to say, too many solid Christian families who faithfully attend church and love God open their homes to this kind of heartache every time they turn on the television and allow the media to flood their minds with every kind of advertisement and program imaginable that can barely pass censorship. Watching television on a daily basis causes us to become numb and immune to the perverse things that the world has to offer. I am just simply saying that a powerful line needs to be drawn. Purity is on one side, and perverseness is on the other. It has to be crystal clear what will be allowed and what will not be allowed. Christians cannot live a duplicitous life.

5. I dream for our children that they would always know the fullness of God's blessings. *"That our garners may be full, affording all manner of store: that our sheep may bring forth thousands and ten thousands in our streets."* (Psalm 144:13) Young people should always know the fullness of God's blessings—not the edge. Personally, I do not want to see how *little* of God I can get by with. How much Bible do I **have** to read? Do I **have** to pray today? I don't want to live on the edge of

God's blessings. I want to be smack dab in the fullness of God's blessings!

6. I dream for our children that they would know the happiness that comes from hard work and obedience and the contentment that comes from gratitude. *"Happy is that people, that is in such a case: yea, happy is that people, whose God is the LORD."* (Psalm 144:15) I grew up in a home where we did not have much money for a long time. Dad wasn't a businessman at first; he was a common laborer making minimal wages. Our car was a big, brown, ugly 1952 Chevrolet with a green interior. The car didn't have a muffler, so it had lots of pizzazz! We had to keep that car for a long time.

Whenever my mother would get in the car, she would look over the backseat at me, and she would say, "Isn't this the greatest car in all the world? Don't you just love our 'Brown Bomber'?"

This totally underpowered car would barely crest a hill, and my mother would say, "What an awesome car!"

And you know what? I believed her! Our "Brown Bomber" was the best! I grew up a happy, contented boy because I grew up with happy, contented parents who derived their happiness from working hard, obeying God, and being grateful for everything we had.

We must dedicate ourselves afresh to the cause of servant leadership so that the next generation will grow up secure, confident, stable, blessed, and happy. We must give them a fighting chance in a perverse and wicked world.

Afterword

People who are pursuing something beyond success—who are engaged in making an impact on the world—want to leave a legacy that continues after them. Perhaps no one has expressed this commitment more passionately than the playwright, George Bernard Shaw:

This is the true joy in life, the being recognized by yourself as a mighty one; the being thoroughly worn out before you are thrown on the scrap heap; the being a force of nature instead of a feverish selfish little clod of ailments and grievances complaining that the world will not devote itself to making you happy.

I am of the opinion that my life belongs to the whole community and as long as I live, it is my privilege to do for it whatever I can. I want to be thoroughly used up when I die, for the harder I work, the more I live.

I rejoice in life for its own sake. Life is no brief candle to me. It is a sort of splendid torch which I have got hold of for the moment, and I want to make it burn as brightly as possible before handing it on to future generations.[1]

The legacy that must be left by today's leaders for future generations is one of servant leadership. That heritage of servant leadership is serving others as Jesus did.

End Notes

[1]Harold Myra and Marshall Shelley, *The Leadership Secrets of Billy Graham* (Grand Rapids: Zondervan, 2005), 26-27. [Theodore Roosevelt's "arena" statement is perhaps the most famous quotation on the subject of leadership.]

INTRODUCTION

[1]Warren Bennis and Burt Nannus, *Leaders: The Strategies for Taking Charge* (New York: Harper & Row Publishers, 1985), 4-5.

[2]Joseph L. Badaracco, Jr., *Leading Quietly: An Unorthodox Guide to Doing the Right Thing* (Boston: Harvard Business School Press, 2002), 34.

[3]Col. Larry R. Donnithorne, Ret., *The West Point Way of Leadership: From Learning Principled Leadership to Practicing It* (New York: Currency and Doubleday, 1993), 19.

[4]Harrison Owen, *The Spirit of Leadership: Liberating the Leader in Each of Us* (San Francisco: Berrett-Koehler Publishers, Inc., 1999), 61.

[5] Harold S. Geneen, "Leadership," in *The Book of Leadership Wisdom: Classic Writings by Legendary Business Leaders* ed. by Peter Krass (New York: John Wiley & Sons, Inc., 1998), 3.

[6] Robert W. Galvin, "Real Leaders Create Industries," in *The Book of Leadership Wisdom*, 1998.

[7] Zig Ziglar, *Top Performance: How to Develop Excellence in Yourself and Others* (Old Tappan: Fleming H. Revell Company, 1986), 31.

[8] William A. Cohen, *The Art of the Leader* (Englewood Cliffs: Prentice Hall, 1990), 9.

[9] Bennis and Nannus, 188.

[10] Max DuPree, *Leadership Is an Art* (New York: Bantam Doubleday Dell Publishing Group, Inc., 1989), 3.

[11] LeRoy Eims, *Be the Leader You Were Meant to Be: Biblical Principles of Leadership* (Wheaton: Victor Books, 1987), 55.

[12] Chris Roebuck, *Effective Leadership* (New York: Marshall Editions Developments, LTD, 1999), 51.

[13] John C. Maxwell, *The 21 Irrefutable Laws of Leadership* (Nashville: Thomas Nelson Publishers, 1998), 17.

[14] Norman L. Frigon, Sr. & Harry K. Jackson, Jr. *The Leader: Developing the Skills and Personal Qualities You Need to Lead Effectively* (New York: American Management Association, 1996), 16.

[15] Dale Carnegie and Associates, Inc., *The Leader in You: How to Win Friends, Influence People, and Succeed in a Changing World* (New York: Simon and Schuster, 1993), 22.

[16] Ken Blanchard, "Leading at a Higher Level," in *Leading at a Higher Level: Blanchard on Leadership and Creating High Performing Organizations* ed. by The Founding Associates and Consulting Partners of the Ken Blanchard Companies (Upper Saddle River: Prentice Hall, 2007), xix.

[17] Eims, 7.

[18] David Handler, "Electing to Lead," *Quick Printing*, Vol. 31, No. 4 (January 2009), 28.

[19] DuPree, 12.

[20] Ken Blanchard, Scott Blanchard, and Drea Zigarmi, "Servant Leadership," in *Leading at a Higher Level*, 249.

[21] Eims, 41.

Chapter One
SERVANT LEADERSHIP

[1] Ken Blanchard, "Foreword: The Heart of Servant Leadership," in *Focus on Leadership: Servant Leadership for the Twenty-First Century*, ed. by Larry C. Spears and Michelle Lawrence (New York: John Wiley and Sons, Inc., 2002), xi.

[2] Ken Blanchard, "Foreword: The Heart of Servant Leadership," in *Focus on Leadership*, ix.

[3] Robert K. Greenleaf, *Servant Leadership: A Journey Into the Nature of Legitimate Power and Greatness* (New York: Paulist Press, 1977), 13.

[4] Bennis and Nannus, 1-2.

[5] Max Dupree, "Servant Leadership: Three Things Necessary," in *Focus on Leadership*, 91.

[6]Ken Blanchard, "Foreword: The Heart of Servant Leadership," in *Focus on Leadership*, xi.

[7]Henri J. M. Nouwen, *In the Name of Jesus: Reflections on Christian Leadership* (New York: The Crossroad Publishing Co., 1989), 63.

[8]Ziglar, 30.

[9]Hamilton Beazley and Julie Beggs, "Teaching Servant Leadership," in *Focus on Leadership*, 58.

[10]Roebuck, 27.

[11]Ken Blanchard, Scott Blanchard, and Drea Zigarmi, "Servant Leadership," in *Leading at a Higher Level*, 263-64.

Chapter 2
EXERCISING THE MIND IN SERVANT LEADERSHIP
[1]Max Dupree, *Leadership Is an Art*, 68.

Chapter 3
THE STEPS TO BECOMING A SERVANT LEADER
[1]John C. Maxwell, *Developing the Leaders Around You: How to Help Others Reach Their Full Potential* (Nashville, Thomas Nelson Publishers, 1995), 24.

[2]Eims, 65.

[3]Myra and Shelley, 201.

[4]Myra and Shelley, 203.

[5]Ziglar, 44.

[6]Eims, 24.

Chapter 4
COMPREHENDING CRITICISM
[1] Myra and Shelley, 79.

[2] Ziglar, 89.

[3] Myra and Shelley, 59.

[4] Myra and Shelley, 89.

Chapter 5
DEVELOPING THE CHARACTER OF CHRIST
[1] Donnitorne, 165.

[2] Frigon, Sr., and Jackson, Jr., 32.

[3] John Adair, *How to Grow Leaders: The Seven Key Principles of Effective Leadership* (Sterling: Kogan Page Limited, 2005), 105.

Chapter 6
THE SPIRIT OF SERVANT LEADERSHIP
[1] John C. Maxwell, *Developing the Leaders Around You*, 14.

[2] Bennis and Mannus, 62-63.

[3] DuPree, 13.

[4] John Maxwell, *The 21 Irrefutable Laws of Leadership*, 189.

[5] Andrew Murray, *The Prayer Life* (Chicago: Moody Press, n.d.), 88.

[6] Richard Pfeiffer, *Creating Real Relationships* (New York: Growth Publishing, 1999), 91.

[7] Ken Blanchard and Margret McBride, *The One-Minute Apology: A Powerful Way to Make Things Better* (New York: HarperCollins Publishers, Inc., 2003), 77.

Chapter 7
THE INSECURITY OF THE SERVANT FOLLOWER
[1] Jack Hyles, *Exploring Prayer With Jack Hyles* (Hammond: Hyles-Anderson Publishers, 1983), 110-16.

Chapter 8
THE CHALLENGES OF SERVANT LEADERSHIP
[1] Myra and Shelley, 187.
[2] Nouwen, 45.
[3] Myra and Shelley, 187.
[4] Myra and Shelley, 76.

Chapter 9
THE LANGUAGE OF LEADERSHIP TO FOLLOWSHIP
[1] Greenleaf, 227.
[2] Maxwell, *Developing the Leaders Around You*, 65.
[3] Dr. Les Parrott and Leslie Parrott, *Relationships: An Open and Honest Guide to Making Bad Relationships Better and Good Relationships Great* (Grand Rapids: Zondervan Publishing House, 1998), 63.

[4] Carnegie, 90.

[5] Robert Abel, *The Relationship Toolbox: Tools for Love, Healing and Personal Empowerment* (Denver: Valentine Publishing House, 1998), 145.

[6] Dr. Henry Cloud and Dr. John Townsend, *21 Days to a Great Marriage: A Grownup Approach to Couplehood* (Nashville: Integrity House, 2006), 174.

[7] Alan Loy McGinnis, *The Friendship Factor* (Minneapolis: Augsburg Publishing House, 1979), 103-04.

[8] H. Norman Wright, *Helping Those Who Hurt: How to Be There for Your Friends in Need* (Bloomington, Minn.: Bethany House Publishers, 2003), 39.

[9] Leo Buscaglia, *Loving Each Other: The Challenge of Human Relationships* (New York: Holt, Rinehart and Winston, 1984), 65.

[10] McGinnis, 114.

[11] Susan Campbell, Ph.D., *Saying What's Real: 7 Keys to Authentic Communication and Relationship Success* (Tiburon, Calif.: An H. J. Kramer Book, 2005), 85.

[12] Buscaglia, 184.

[13] Dr. Rick Brinkman and Dr. Rick Kirschner, *Dealing With People You Can't Stand: How to Bring Out the Best in People at Their Worst* (New York: McGraw-Hill, Inc., 1994), 44.

[14] John C. Maxwell, *Developing the Leaders Around You*, 67.

[15] Myra and Shelley, 130.

[16] Ken Blanchard, William Oncken, Jr., and Hal Barrows, *The One-Minute Manager Meets the Monkey* (New York: Blanchard Family Partnership, 1989), 73.

[17] Donnithorne, 159.

[18] Rupert Eales-White, *How to Be a Better Leader* (London: Kogan Page Limited, 1988), 46.

[19] Myra and Shelley, 134.

[20] Carnegie, 137-38.

[21] Ziglar, 110.

[22] Donnithore, 97.

[23] DuPree, 11.

[24] The Founding Associates and Consulting Partners of the Ken Blanchard Companies, xx.

[25] Myra and Shelley, 205.

[26] Ken Blanchard, Scott Blanchard, and Drea Zigarmi, "Servant Leadership" in *Leading at a Higher Level*, 276.

Chapter 10
MAKING YOUR FOLLOWERS

[1] Frigon, Sr., and Jackson, Jr., viii.

[2] Andrew S. Grove, "Taking the Hype Out of Leadership," quoted in *The Book of Leadership Wisdom*, 25.

[3] Dupree, 12.

[4] Myra and Shelley, 131.

[5] Bill George, *Authentic Leadership: Rediscovering the Secrets to Creating Lasting Value* (San Francisco, Jossey Bros., 2003), 19.

[6] Scott Campbell & Ellen Samiec, *5-D Leadership: Key Dimensions for Leading in the Real World* (Mountain View, Calif.: Davies-Black Publishing, 2005), 40.

[7] Ken Blanchard, Scott Blanchard, & Drea Zigarmi, "Servant Leadership," in *Leading at a Higher Level*, 270-71.

[8] *A Voice: The Quotations of Dr. Jack Hyles* (Hammond, Ind.: Lapina Publications, 2000), 78.

Chapter 11
WHAT I DREAM FOR OUR CHILDREN
[1] Ziglar, 24.
[2] Ziglar, 230.
[3] Carnegie, 86.

AFTERWORD
[1] Tracy Goss, *The Last Word on Power: Executive Re-invention for Leaders Who Must Make the Impossible Happen* (New York: A Currency Book Published by Doubleday, 1996), 5.

Sources Consulted

Abel, Robert. *The Relationship Toolbox: Tools for Love, Healing and Personal Empowerment*. Denver: Valentine Publishing House, 1998.

Adair, John. *How to Grow Leaders: The Seven Key Principles of Effective Leadership*. Sterling: Kogan Page Ltd., 2005.

A Voice: The Quotations of Dr. Jack Hyles. Hammond, Ind.: Lapina Publications, 2000.

Badaracco, Jr., Joseph L. *Leading Quietly: An Unorthodox Guide to Doing the Right Thing*. Boston: Harvard Business School Press, 2002.

Baldoni, John. *How Great Leaders Get Great Results*. New York: McGraw Hill Companies, 2006.

Bennis, Warren and Burt Nannus. *Leaders: The Strategies for Taking Charge*. New York: Harper & Row Publishers, 1985.

Blanchard, Ken and Margret McBride. *The One-Minute Apology: A Powerful Way to Make Things Better*. New York: HarperCollins Publishers, Inc., 2003.

Blanchard, Ken, William Oncken, Jr., and Hal Barrows. *The One-Minute Manager Meets the Monkey*. New York: Blanchard Family Partnership, 1989.

Blank, Warren. *The 9 Natural Laws of Leadership*. New York: Amacom, 1995.

Brinkman, Dr. Rick and Dr. Rick Kirschner. *Dealing With People You Can't Stand*. New York: McGraw-Hill, Inc., 1994.

Buscaglia, Leo. *Loving Each Other: The Challenge of Human Relationships*. New York: Holt, Rinehart and Winston, 1984.

Campbell, Scott and Ellen Samiec. *5-D Leadership*. Mountain View, Calif.: Davies-Black Publishing, 2005.

Campbell, Ph.D., Susan. *Saying What's Real: 7 Keys to Authentic Communication and Relationship Success*. Tiburon, Calif.: An H. J. Kramer Book, 2005.

Carnegie, Dale and Associates, Inc. *The Leader in You: How to Win Friends, Influence People, and Succeed in a Changing World*. New York: Simon and Schuster, 1993.

Cloud, Dr. Henry and Dr. John Townsend. *21 Days to a Great Marriage*. Nashville: Integrity House, 2006.

Cohen, William A. *The Art of the Leader*. Englewood Cliffs: Prentice Hall, 1990.

Cohen, William A. *The Stuff of Leaders: The Eight Universal Laws of Leadership*. Marietta: Longstreet, 1998.

Donnithorne, Ret. Col. Larry R. *The West Point Way of Leadership: From Learning Principled Leadership to Practicing It*. New York: Currency and Doubleday, 1993.

DuPree, Max. *Leadership Is an Art*. New York: Bantam Doubleday Dell Publishing Group, Inc., 1989.

Eales-White, Rupert. *How to Be a Better Leader*. London: Kogan Page Limited, 1988.

Eims, LeRoy. *Be the Leader You Were Meant to Be: Biblical Principles of Leadership*. Wheaton: Victor Books, 1987.

The Founding Associates and Consulting Partners of the Ken Blanchard Companies. *Leading at a Higher Level: Blanchard on Leadership and Creating High Performing Organizations*. Upper Saddle River: Prentice Hall, 2007.

Frigon, Sr., Norman L. and Harry K. Jackson, Jr. *The Leader: Developing the Skills and Personal Qualities You Need to Lead Effectively*. New York: American Management Association, 1996.

George, Bill. *Authentic Leadership: Rediscovering the Secrets to Creating Lasting Value*. San Francisco, Jossey Bros., 2003.

Godin, Seth. *Wisdom, Inc.: 26 Business Virtues That Turn Ordinary People Into Extraordinary Leaders*. New York: Harper Collins Publishers, Inc., 1995.

Goss, Tracy. *The Last Word on Power: Executive Re-invention for Leaders Who Must Make the Impossible Happen*. New York: A Currency Book Published by Doubleday, 1996.

Greenleaf, Robert K. *Servant Leadership: A Journey Into the Nature of Legitimate Power and Greatness*. New York: Paulist Press, 1977.

Handler, David. "Electing to Lead." *Quick Printing*. Vol. 31, No. 4. January 2009.

Hyles, Jack. *Exploring Prayer With Jack Hyles*. Hammond: Hyles-Anderson Publishers, 1983.

Krass, Peter, ed. *The Book of Leadership Wisdom: Classic Writings by Legendary Business Leaders*. New York: John Wiley & Sons, Inc., 1998.

Mackoff, Barbara and Gary Wenet. *The Inner Walk of Leaders: Leadership as a Habit of Mind*. New York: Amacom, 2001.

Maxwell, John C. Maxwell. *Developing the Leaders Around You: How to Help Others Reach Their Potential*. Nashville, Thomas Nelson Publishers, 1995.

Maxwell, John C. *The 21 Irrefutable Laws of Leadership*. Nashville: Thomas Nelson Publishers, 1998.

McGinnis, Alan Loy. *The Friendship Factor*. Minneapolis: Augsburg Publishing House, 1979.

Murray, Andrew. *The Prayer Life*. Chicago: Moody Press, n.d.

Myra, Harold and Marshall Shelley. *The Leadership Secrets of Billy Graham*. Grand Rapids: Zondervan, 2005.

Nouwen, Henri J. M. *In the Name of Jesus: Reflections on Christian Leadership*. New York: The Crossroad Publishing Co., 1989.

Owen, Harrison. *The Spirit of Leadership: Liberating the Leader in Each of Us*. San Francisco: Berrett-Koehler Publishers, Inc., 1999.

Parrott, Dr. Les and Leslie Parrott. *Relationships: An Open and Honest Guide to Making Bad Relationships Better and Good Relationships Great*. Grand Rapids: Zondervan Publishing House, 1998.

Pfeiffer, Richard. *Creating Real Relationships*. New York: Growth Publishing, 1999.

Roebuck, Chris. *Effective Leadership*. New York: Marshall Editions Developments, Ltd., 1999.

Spears, Larry C. and Michelle Lawrence, ed. *Focus on Leadership: Servant Leadership for the Twenty-First Century*. New York: John Wiley and Sons, Inc., 2002.

Wright, H. Norman Wright. *Helping Those Who Hurt: How to Be There for Your Friends in Need*. Bloomington, Minn.: Bethany House Publishers, 2003.

Ziglar, Zig. *Top Performance: How to Develop Excellence in Yourself and Others*. Old Tappan: Fleming H. Revell Company, 1986.